A Modest Proposal for Peace, Prosperity, and Happiness

A Modest Proposal

Proposal

For Peace, Prosperity And Happiness

FRANKY SCHAEFFER
HAROLD FICKETT

Thomas Nelson Publishers   Nashville • Camden • New York

Published in Nashville, Tennessee, by Thomas Nelson, Inc. and distributed in Canada by Lawson Falle, Ltd., Cambridge, Ontario.

Excerpts on pp. 142-145 from introduction to *The Resourceful Earth: A Response to Global 2000,* copyright © 1984 by Julian L. Simon and Herman Kahn. Reprinted by permission of Basil Blackwell, Inc., New York.

Illustrations by Jerry Tiritilli.

Interior and cover design by Sarah Cioni/Cioni Artworks.

Printed in the United States of America.

ISBN 0-8407-5407-8

For Jessica, Francis, John Lewis, and Hal

THE BUREAU OF POPULATION
AND ENVIRONMENT
14815 PENNSYLVANIA AVE.
WASHINGTON, D.C.
00100-DF-XXXY3420

June 18, 1992

Ms. Diana Marsh
Special Assistant to the Undersecretary
The Bureau of Population and Environment
14815 Pennsylvania Avenue, Washington, D.C.
0010-DF-XXXY3420

Dear Di:

Our lunch together last Wednesday was such a pleasure that I am being so bold as to enclose for your review my labor of love, <u>A</u> Modest <u>Proposal</u> <u>For</u> Peace, <u>Prosperity,</u> and Happiness. I don't have to tell you what a wasp's nest of egotists makes up our elected government, or sketch the personality profile of the common civil servant who lives in cozy symbiosis with them. You understand our political world as well or better than anyone. That's why our lunch was an absolute delight. I have rarely had the opportunity of talking with someone so <u>thoughtful</u> about the job we should be doing in the government. I felt immediately that you were, if I may say so, a sympathetic spirit. I take this liberty because, while your station is far above mine, you made me feel that we were truly colleagues, equals engaged in a high endeavor. Your influence in this regard has had an impact on the whole bureau; I've talked to many people from the treasury and other governmental departments who envy our egalitarian <u>modus vivendi.</u> I know that as your power increases—which it certainly will—this unity of mind and heart will grow stronger.

Unhappily even those of us in the Bureau still live east of Eden. Part of the reason that I am sending my manuscript to you, in this informal way, comes from the personality conflict that inevitably, it seems, pits my immediate superior, Charles Hunt, against me. As I have a DPL 5 ranking he cannot, of course, seriously threaten my job security; but he <u>has</u> been successful, I'm sorry to say, in thwarting my efforts on every hand. I know that by going outside the usual channels in sending my latest study for the Bureau to you I run the risk of censure. And indeed if you choose to view my action in an unfavorable light, I can only recognize the justice of your judgment and ask your forgiveness. I feel, however, that the times in which we live are so desperate that the least among us must be willing to sacrifice decorum for the sake of truth. Particularly at just this moment.

While we must not participate in partisan politics, we in the Bureau cannot be unaware that the present member of the Oval Office (or orifice, as I am sometimes tempted to say) has chosen to treat the Bureau of Population and Environment as if it did not exist. We must hope that the coming presidential election will bring another party into power so that we may do more than twiddle our thumbs. (And it looks as if this may well come to pass.) As the highest ranking civil servant in the department, you will be in a key position to influence policy. Many of the reforms we should be advocating, as they are found in my Proposal, will need to be administered by complex bureaucracies. No one appointed to head the Bureau can be expected to understand all the reasons we need these feedback-adaptive systems, much less understand the systems themselves. Many of us have made this our life work, after all, and have been constructing the infrastructure of population management for decades. The newly appointed secretary of the Bureau then will be—not to put too fine a point on it—an amateur, and he will no doubt rely to a great extent on you for direction. For this reason I have taken the grave risk of sending my Proposal to you outside of regular channels.

Yet by no means do I present this Proposal to you as the last word. It is still in a very rough stage of composition. The concluding sections in particular represent a very tentative and qualified exploration of questions which deserve a great deal of further study. If you will take the time to give me your honest critique, I would consider that the highest of compliments. For again, the dialectic of our give and take over lunch encouraged me so much, to the extent that I felt I might, as your subaltern, participate in the process that will enable us to find remedies for the many ills afflicting the world's population. It goes without saying, I'm sure, that this document is FOR YOUR EYES ONLY. Any leak of the contents to the general public might cause a wholly unnecessary flap.

I know you will need some time to read and digest this, but in the meantime I would appreciate some word about whether or not you consider this gesture appropriate. Of course if you find another opening on you calendar, I would be only too happy to have lunch with you again and discuss the matter upon that most convivial occasion.

All the best,

C.B. Train

C.B. Train
Research Associate

A MODEST PROPOSAL

FOR PEACE, PROSPERITY AND HAPPINESS

C.B. TRAIN

RESEARCH ASSOCIATE
THE BUREAU OF POPULATION AND ENVIRONMENT
JUNE 18, 1992

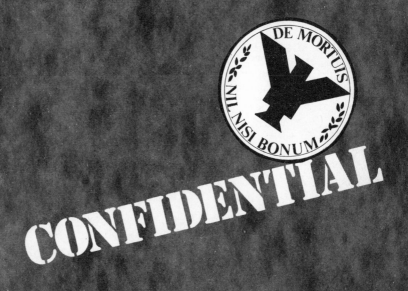

DE MORTUIS
NIL NISI BONUM

CONFIDENTIAL

Contents

Who in this last decade of the twentieth century can avoid feeling that we live in apocalyptic times? Having disregarded our prophets, the futurists of the last three decades, we are daily confronted, in these early years of the 1990s, with the catastrophic events they predicted. The data presently available must finally convince any reasonable person that our own Four Horsemen—famine, pollution, war, and overpopulation—are bearing down hard upon us. Until now we have acted as if these forces were as inexplicable in their movements as the four winds. Soon, however, the vicious cycle which we ourselves set in motion will catch up with us. And we will reap the whirlwind. What a terrible retribution it may be.

Famine. Our world is hungry. At least half of its inhabitants are undernourished or malnourished.[1] Famine has become not so much a dreaded visitation as the very context of life for over one billion men, women, and children. The peoples of the sub-Sahara regions in Africa, subsistence farmers clinging to life high up in the Himalayan hills of Asia, and the squatters in shantytowns about Rio, Bogota, and Lima—these groups and many others live in constant and unspeakable misery. Millions die each year of starvation; the U.N. Economic and Social Commission for Asia and the Pacific has predicted that "500 million starvation deaths [will have occurred] between 1980 and 2025."[2] In addition, thirty-five thousand children die *per day* from infectious diseases that prove fatal only because of the victims' malnourished condition.[3] Malaria and other such banes, once thought practically eliminated, have made all too marked comebacks. Malnutrition

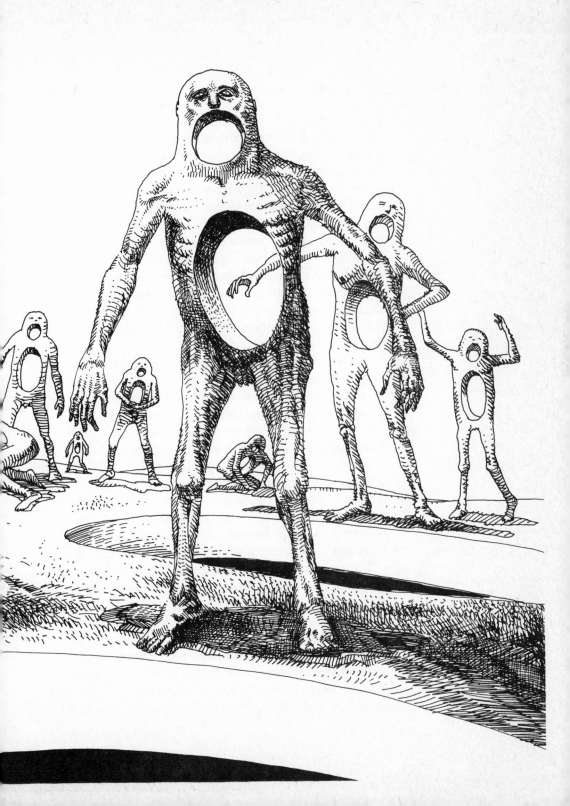

itself *causes* such diseases as kwashiorkor, which sears the bodies of its victims with horrible signs of its cause. Open sores spread over the victim's flesh, particularly on the thighs and lower body, so that its sufferers look as if they have been badly burned.

Hunger also has less visible but no less devastating effects. The world's hungry billions lack protein more than anything else in their diets. This nutritional deficit often dwarfs, cripples, and blinds the offspring of the poor; it also causes mental retardation. There is very little hope for improvement in these conditions, since the real price of food has increased by more than 60 percent in the last twenty years and continues to climb.[4]

The world's hungry billions are also subjected to a famine of services just as crucial to health as food. Poor sanitation causes acute health problems of pandemic proportions. One-third of the world does not have adequate waste disposal facilities. One-fourth of urban populations and nine-tenths of the population in underdeveloped countries (UDCs) lack safe latrines or sewage disposal systems. Untreated human wastes cause many diseases, such as, to take just one example, schistosomiasis, a debilitating parasitic disease which, at last count, afflicts 200 million people in seventy-one countries.[5]

The world's hungry are also thirsty. Sixty-two percent of those in UDCs do not have access to enough clean water.[6]

Nor do they have ready access to the simplest of fuels to cook whatever meager supplies of food they manage to attain. Indians are forced to burn dung, stealing much-needed nutrients from their farming land. In the arid Sahel of Africa, the energies of one person in each family must be devoted full-time to wood gathering. Charcoal prices in one central Sudanian town tripled in the seventies and have continued to rise. West Africans spend one-fourth of their income on fuel wood, as well.[7]

All of these hardships exist in a world in which many of the biggest health problems in developed nations—cardiovascular disease among them—derive from obesity; a world in which Americans spend hundreds of millions of dollars feeding their pets the very proteins that would spare hungry children from going blind or becoming crippled.

Indeed, all of these problems are exacerbated by the refusal on the part of some developed nations to regulate their economies. The so-called "free-enterprise" system rests on the backs of the poor in UDCs who provide cheap labor and the resources of their nations to the industrial machine of the Western world. That machine keeps these workers in grinding poverty while it increases the wealth of the developed nations, most particularly the fiduciary elite who control the international marketplace.

Pollution. The second horseman, pollution, has come upon us today in ways as multitudinous as locust in a time of plague. Since we are concerned here with basic human needs, we shall concentrate on pollution issues that pose the most serious threats to humankind's well-being. Most of these concerns relate to the uses of arable land and the consumption of our energy resources.

Since that seminal work, *Losing Ground* by Eckholm in 1976, we have all known that the acreage of arable land around the globe is decreasing.[8] One million hectares are lost to urbanization, highways, strip mining, and similar uses each year.[9] A crop

The first four billion years of evolutionary development left the earth a beautifully rich, infinitely intricate and wondrously complex organism. In less than one hundred years, a cosmic eyeblink, evolution's crowning achievement has proven to be her biggest mistake.

area as large as the state of Nebraska has been paved over since World War II.[10] At the same time much of the land we cultivate or give over to grazing has so deteriorated that deserts around the world are expanding their borders, claiming the territories millions of people depend upon for their livelihood. The Sahara, for instance, grows at the rate of 650,000 acres per year.[11] Worldwide this process of "desertification" renders useless, annually, an area the size of Maine.[12] By U.N. estimates, 78 million people, at last count, lived in areas that have already become wastelands. There are many immediate causes: erosion, overgrazing, loss of organic matter, salinization, alkalinization, and waterlogging. All of these, however, speak of simple overuse. These lands are being ravaged by population plague. But more about that later.

The "solutions" we have found to this problem simply compound it. The ideology of the much-touted "Green Revolution" held that the world could once again become a paradise of abundance through fertilizers derived from petroleum. These fertilizers, however, are expensive, and therefore are not obtainable by those most in need—the world's poor. Also, they raise expectations about the yield of an average acre so much that farmers in the developed countries have thrown caution to the wind and are producing yields that can only be maintained through the use of increasing amounts of such fertilizers. All the while, of course, the nu-trients belonging to the land itself are becoming more and more depleted. The denitrification (reduc-tion of nitrites and nitrates) of these fertilizers pro-duces emissions which pose a grave threat to the ozone layer of the earth's atmosphere, as well. The ozone layer plays a crucial role in screening the world's food crop from an excessive amount of ultraviolet rays from the sun. To weaken this shield may prove disastrous to the protection of human life, because, to put it simply, what we put in the ground to nourish our crops will soon, if it is not already doing so, virtually incinerate those same crops by exposing them to too many ultraviolet rays when they reach the surface.

Finally, the Green Revolution has also introduced superstrains of wheat and other grains which increase the land's yield per acre. These genetically engineered crops are monocultures, which often do not have enough genetic diversity to resist pests found in various locales. They have become particularly susceptible to pestilence since more and more insects have become resistant to the pesticides that are also a part of the Green Revolution's cache of weapons. The corn blight of 1971, the antra bug explosion of 1985, and last year's (1991) "burn-off" crop failure ratio all attest to these grim realities.

The destruction of so much arable land from various pollutants has put increasing pressure on the world's forests, huge acreages being converted to agricultural and other uses. The world's forests are disappearing at the alarming rate of 18-20 million hectares a year, an area as large as Northern California.[13] In 1980 it was projected that, by the year 2000, 40 percent of the remaining forest cover in underdeveloped nations would be gone.[14] At the midpoint of this prediction, that figure looks to hold up. Even so, at first thought, we might not lament this phenomenon. The tropical forests of Africa, Asia, and South America would seem to provide much needed new ground for our expanding needs. But we must remember that these "green belts," along with diatomic planktons found in the ocean (whose populations are decimated by oil spills, the incidence of which is increasing), account for more than 70 percent of the world's oxygen. What appetite will we have for the products of these regions when we find ourselves gasping for breath?

Furthermore, though capable of supporting the lush flora and fauna of their ecosystems, the great tropical forests do *not* have the rich, deep layer of topsoil which grains and other staple crops demand. Much of the Himalayas, Andes, and East African highlands have been cleared of trees to extend agriculture. These efforts have been to little purpose other than giving false hope to people who must yearly occupy higher and higher terrain to carry on their subsistence farming. The soil they are cultivating might be enriched for a time by the techniques of the Green Revolution, it's true; but it would be the cruelest cheat to help those who live in these areas produce the abundance our petroleum reserves might create when we know these reserves will soon be exhausted. The soil of these regions would then be even less capable of supporting life than it would normally.

Yet such a deception would be in accord with our own willful blindness to the scarcity of that relatively clean fossil fuel, petroleum, and the pollution hazards posed by its trashy cousin, coal. The world, and the United States in particular, is intent on "business as usual" while the read-out on the gas tank approaches zero. We have now burned about three-quarters of the earth's total reserves of oil, or 1,500 billion of the world's original endowment of 2,000 billion barrels. Ninety percent of those barrels consumed have been used in the last thirty-five years.[15] At this rate of consumption, all known reserves will be exhausted within the next fifteen years. Indeed in the last five years oil production has declined from its peak in 1987 because of failing reserves.

Some still have hopes of developing economical methods of extracting oil from shale. The clock is running out on this path of research, however. It is also the explicit and, in my view, tragic policy of the United States to rely in the next decades on coal as the alternative energy source of first choice. While we do have, at the present rate of consumption, abundant coal supplies for a hundred years or more, the use of coal will only exacerbate the problems that the use of oil has brought within a most frightening proximity. No one doubts anymore that the various uses of petroleum have not only depleted the ozone layer, as we have seen, but have also raised the carbon dioxide level in the atmosphere as well.

Already we may be experiencing climatic changes attributable to the Greenhouse Effect, which is the tendency of carbon dioxide in the atmosphere to act as a barrier preventing the earth from emitting heat back toward space. The warmth of the sun enters the atmosphere as it always has, but as the carbon dioxide level goes up, less and less of that warmth is allowed to escape back into space from our atmosphere. The latest estimates project that in the next fifty years the earth will experience a median temperature rise of four degrees. This will not melt the polar ice caps, as was previously feared, but it will raise the level of the ocean by dramatically increasing snowfall at the poles and

Duty, honor, Country. The benediction
of five star generals satisfying their
appetites for the annihilation of our
posterity. The borderlines change, the flags
change as do portraits gracing the currencies,
but the song remains the same.

the subsequent amount of water run-off.[16] That Mayor Blasingame of New York is now advocating that Manhattan extend the borders of its downtown business section through landfills and dikes reminiscent of those used in the Netherlands should awaken us to the clear and present danger of the Greenhouse Effect.[17] Yet this nation is committed to changing, "if it ever has to," as the president says, from one fossil fuel to another, *which will greatly increase the rate at which carbon dioxide accumulates in the atmosphere beyond the present manifestly dangerous levels.* Such madness should be hard to credit if it were not the work of politicians.

Great strides have been made in the development of solar, wind, and geothermal power. Biomass crops are supplementing our domestic supplies of gasoline and other light fuels. The development of the first nuclear fusion reactor—fusion being a much "cleaner" process than fission—may be close at hand. But the international energy cartel (that compound of avaricious international oil companies, venal sheiks, and fat middlemen) has adopted a policy of encouraging consumption so conspicuous that convulsive symptoms must appear in the body politic despite these advances.

War. The disparity between the wealthy nations and those they exploit makes local wars fought over declining resources virtually inevitable. These regional conflicts, in turn, make the possibility of a thermonuclear holocaust ever more likely. What happens when famines wipe out those delicate monoculture crops in underdeveloped nations, and the agricultural machine of the developed nations no longer has the fuel to export massive amounts of grain? What happens when the developing nations realize famines in their countries have occurred in part because of our pollution of the "global commons"—the earth's atmosphere? Of the world's 200 river basins, 148 are shared by two or more countries, and 52 of these 148 are shared by three to ten countries.[18] What happens when the requirements for water double, as they are predicted to, in half the nations of the world? Brazil and Argentina have always quarreled over the Plata River. Syria and Iraq have had long standing disputes over the Euphrates, and the bloodshed between Bangladesh and India over the Ganges should still be fresh and chillingly bright in the public mind. What happens when at least half the world becomes embroiled in such disputes?

It is clear that the synergistic combination of gross economic inequities between the developed and the underdeveloped nations, and the pollution hazards threatening the lives of the people in both must, if history is any guide, result in worldwide conflict. And who can fail to imagine another Idi Amin, or Khadafy, or Quizo resorting to nuclear terrorism to obtain food and materials for his starving people?[19] Will we, we might well ask, be above resorting to nuclear threats in order to extract the natural resources we depend on? The quarter of the world's inhabitants who live in developed nations take unto themselves three-fourths of the world's mineral production.[20] While one-fifteenth of the world's population lives in the United States, America controls one-third of the world's wealth.[21] Do we have the self-control necessary to stop gratifying appetites which decades of brain-washing advertising have created? Will the communist nations, so bellig-

Oh earth, fertile garden of the universe, you teem with maggots feeding upon your fruit until they turn upon one another. The cosmos bears silent witness to your savage rape, proclaiming judgment upon your guests: you are far too kind, to the likes of these.

erent in their imagined need for self-protection, become more peace loving in such an atmosphere? The possibilities for conflict are truly frightening.

Overpopulation. In fact, ineluctably, all the people of the world are now caught up in what we might call the economics of despair. The relevance of the fourth horseman—overpopulation and the death it brings—must be plain by now. Our lands are being overused because we have exceeded the human numbers they are capable of supporting. The earth simply does not have the carrying capacity necessary. There are not enough natural resources to go around, and the resources which still exist, particularly those on which the industrial machines of the developed nations depend, are disappearing fast. And yet the developed nations continue to afflict themselves with new cravings for ever more outlandish extravagances, plundering the resources of the underdeveloped nations for their own satisfactions.[22]

We do pay something for these resources; sadly, it is both too much and too little. We have exported just enough wealth (mainly in the form of technology) to lower mortality rates in underdeveloped nations. As a result, the populations of these countries are skyrocketing. But we do not pay enough and are not capable of supplying the wealth (food principally) necessary to support these populations adequately. As a result, the economics of despair is essentially a vicious cycle in which we in the developed nations will have pillaged, and they in the underdeveloped ones will have grown in human numbers, until that certain date when they have nothing to sell and we nothing to pay or give, and five to seven billion people will be at each other's throats. Rat populations subjected to the kind of overcrowding conditions we are approaching become sterile and insane and often carry aggression against their fellows to the very limit: cannibalism.[23] The developed nations of the world are locked with the underdeveloped nations in what must surely prove a death-grip to all of us.

In bringing upon ourselves the death of our overly populated planet, we are without excuse. Since Malthus in the eighteenth century, we have known that the wealth created by a growing population increases by addition, but populations themselves multiply geometrically. We have also understood, or should have, what Malthus called the "dismal theorem": that growing populations will always eat up whatever wealth technological innovations create, so that anything but a replacement fertility rate leads inexorably to a reduced standard of living— and when pursued as aggressively as we have pursued this course, to death on a massive scale.[24]

Our own four horsemen: famine, pollution, war, and overpopulation. Are the horrifying results of their dreadful interplay or synergistic combinations inevitable? No. We can break that vicious cycle through population control. As overpopulation precipitates famines, pollution, and war, so its remedy will banish them from the earth. I realize this may sound like a panacea. But that is only because we have not understood until now what real population control must entail.

We at the Bureau of Population and Environment have been given the responsibility of monitoring issues related to population control and the environment; we have also been charged with the task of advising elected officials on possible responses to these issues. Ordinarily we should simply go about our work, leaving the decisions themselves to the president, the Congress, and the federal court system. But as it happens, we, almost alone, are in the position to enable the U.S. government, its allies, and, through treaties, the rest of the world, to act in this time of crisis for the benefit of all humankind. In addition to responsibilities that are specifically assigned to civil servants in various agencies, everyone in the government has an implicit commission to do all she or he can for the causes of peace, liberty, and justice. Our research plainly confronts us with the challenge of alleviating human suffering through bringing about a just society in our own land, and a world order devoted to the same end. We must do far more than merely advise our government, as if we were neutral observers, indifferent to the cries of the world's poor. We must not feign blindness to the possibilities for good, inherent in the technology (bioengineering) being created by the revolution in our understanding of human biology. Intellectual effort remains ineffectual until it finds expression in activism, and, ultimately, in power. My proposal will thus not only present a vision of things, it will also be a summons to the front lines of humanitarian activity. The Bureau of Population and Environment must choose to play its potentially crucial role in the advance of human history.

We all realize that as much as past visions of a just society have attracted humankind in theory, they have evaded us in practice. But that should not cause us to despair. Reading Thomas More's *Utopia,* Butler's *Erewhon,* and even B. F. Skinner's *Walden II,* we are struck by two things: the ease with which the authors have solved humanity's greatest problems and the fanciful science on which these solutions depend. In the world of people and action, of course, difficulties which submitted to the imagination were recalcitrant to the technology at society's disposal. Now all of life, including life itself, is subject to technique. In bioengineering we have gained the power to bring the utopian vision of every generation into being. All that remains is for the collective mind to attain the will to use its newfound powers. If only we have the daring, each person on the face of the globe will not only have enough to eat and drink, but every resource that he needs to realize his full potential. To each his due: that simple description of justice is a dream as old as humankind itself and as eloquent as Einstein's mathematical definition of energy. When we reflect on all that we are capable of, and, conversely, the imminent disasters to which we may fall victim, we begin to feel the supreme urgency of the moment. This is the high noon of human history. And so I offer the following modest proposal.

We simply must control, as I've indicated, the population—both in the United States and around the world—so that each member of that population can receive his rightful portion of the earth's resources. If we have two apples, two people may have one each. One hundred people, however, will probably tear each other apart in their dispute over who may lay claim to the apples, with the apples themselves being lost in the bargain. Everyone recognizes the undeniable force of this example's logic. Yet because efforts at population control have in the past been carried out for the wrong reasons and in a ruthless fashion, many people will not face up to this issue. After Adolf Hitler's persecution of the Jews in the Holocaust of World War II, the very term *eugenics*—the science that must be the chief instrument of population planning—was not much used from the end of that war until the mid-1980s. In the past few years, however, the stigma of the Nazi brand has largely disappeared. Reasonable people have concluded that our recently acquired knowledge of genetics has utterly changed the complexion of the issues surrounding eugenics.[1]

There has begun to emerge a consensus about how and in what way we should use this new science. Still we must also take into account the objections of those who remain opposed to eugenics. Such a course will not merely be strategically prudent; it will also guide us in how to avoid any misdirection of our true course into the errors of the past. My proposal is thus divided into three stages, each with a set of reforms proper to society's advancement at the time they envision. Stage I calls for provisional population control measures which, lest we court thermonuclear war, must be implemented immediately. In Stage II we will present the forums necessary for the education of the populace in order to prepare it for the adventure of the last measures. These will be undertaken in Stage III, during which society should finally, after its torturous crawl through history, arrive at an ideal stasis.

Stage I simply makes the population control measures we currently employ in a haphazard fashion a matter of conscious policy, coordinated and encouraged by the Bureau of Population and Environment. This is essential if we in the 1990s are to maintain the momentum toward population control generated by the concerns of the seventies and eighties. Indeed, our society is like a man who stutters, pronouncing the first syllable over and over of a word his listener has long since inferred. We need to take the halting messages of our society, standardize them, codify them, and implement them. Further, we need to encourage prophetic voices calling for more far-reaching population control measures.

For instance, in this last half of the twentieth century, we have seen that abortion is very effective medicine in combating population plague. Increasingly sophisticated methods of abortion have now replaced back-alley butchery, thus allowing women reproductive freedom. Vacuum procedures in which the body of the fetus is dismembered are now the methods of choice. For more mature fetuses, of course, dismemberment and removal must be accomplished by the strong and sharp edge of a currette. This D & C-like method often causes patients some discomfort, however. The search for an alternative has produced mixed results. The promise of prostaglandins has faded, as too many of the miscarriages it induces result in live births. Fortunately the much simpler method of introducing a saline solution into the amniotic sac rarely fails. Within minutes or hours the fetus's skin has reddened, blistered, and to a great extent peeled off when it is expelled from the womb. Finally, for very late-term abortions, hysterotomies can be per-

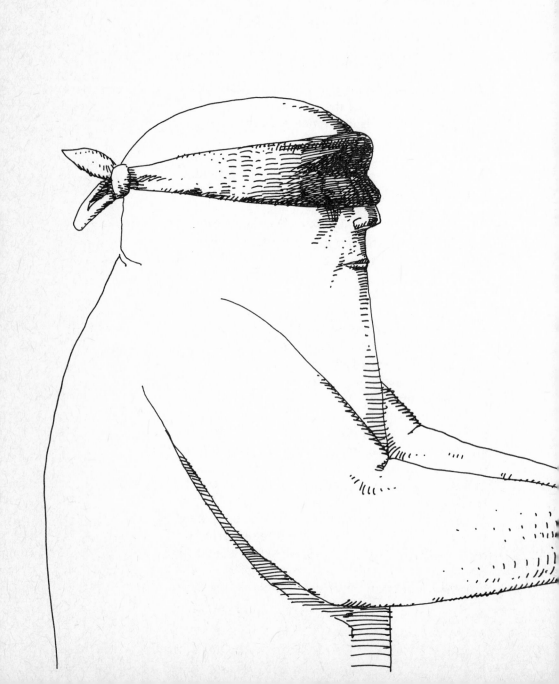

formed, which are no different from caesarean sections except that the fetus is set aside on a table or sent down to the pathology lab to expire, while the physician attends his patient.

While no great hue and cry has been raised about the methods of abortion, like vacuum techniques, in which the fetus is never seen by the uninformed eye, late-term use of the currette and hysterotomies have given people with tender sensibilities pause. Even the attending physicians and nurses are sometimes traumatized by seeing, several times a day, the humanlike shapes of fetal tissue waste.[2] As the *Philadelphia Inquirer* of August 2, 1981, noted, physicians performing this service often "burned out," and their nurses experienced nightmares in which they found themselves trying to hide fetal tissue waste for reasons known only to the subconscious. But as one of the leading physicians of the last decade, Dr. Mildren Hanson, pointed out, many procedures in medicine, like the amputation of a leg, are unpleasant, but the physician has a responsibility not to let his squeamishness interfere with such tasks. Still, since the early eighties, medical schools have very rightly advised sensitive students not to specialize only in gynecological surgery. We don't have to hide this fact, as some champions of reproductive freedom do. We accept that there are many occupations such as the kill chief in a slaughterhouse, in which the repetition of a wholly necessary action becomes dehumanizing. Repetition, itself, is dehumanizing, as those who work in the automobile industry well know. To protest against abortion on the grounds that it might make novice doctors and nurses uncomfortable makes as much sense as arguing against eating meat or driving cars.[3]

That said, abortions do result for many women in problems to which we must supply a psycho-therapeutic solution. Magda Denes, in her book, *In Necessity and Sorrow: Life and Death in an Abortion Hospital,* has addressed the trauma many women, raised in our once misguidedly pro-life culture, have experienced after undergoing an abortion. "Abortions," she says, "are an instance of our exposure. They are heart-rending, ambivalent events of absolute necessity."[4] Most women, it must be admitted, cannot help wondering, even in the worst cases like rape and incest, about the potential life within. Ms. Denes knows their pain, and she has prepared the way for healing by confessing the emotional truth of the matter. That is the first step in any psychotherapeutic cure. What is needful in such cases is the support of those around the once potential mother. These women, who have sacrificed those dreams of potential life, must by all means not be made to feel guilty. They have taken action not only for their own good but for the good of society as well. This must be pointed out to them as often as is necessary. They must be encouraged not to be morbid.

We may also aid future women in their recoveries by adopting the new value-neutral term for abortion, *Fetal Tissue Removal* or *FTR.* The old term, abortion, is still too much associated with coat hanger methods to apply to a procedure that is safer for the mother than birth itself. Apprehension may still attend an FTR procedure, but false guilt should be much reduced. The new term, plus long walks and cups of tea, should set everything to rights, as the British would say.

FTR-on-demand became a reality in the early seventies when the United States Supreme Court, protesting very rightly against accepting one view of when human life begins, decided that viability, the ability to sustain life apart from the mother, should be the criterion for when human life begins. That decision was an absolute watershed in the history of population control. But, as streams and rivers shift their boundaries from year to year, so the demand for population control has shifted the criterion for when human life begins away from "viability." That streambed, if you will, was too shallow. We are on the verge of being able to bring a fetus to what would be its normal term, forty weeks, completely *in vitro,* in test tubes and then those larger containers known as "tumblers." Presently, a fertilized embryo can grow into a mass of hundreds of cells before implantation in a carrier, and can be taken from her at ever earlier dates; the present length of actual maternal gestation needed is down to twelve weeks and dwindling fast. It has turned out that the issue was never when human life begins, but when we shall confer humanity on that life. The crucial question has been seen to be a matter of when the mother (and through her, society) *accepts* the fetus as human. *Acceptability* has replaced *viability* as the criterion for meaningful human life. As a result, the stream of population control has flowed more evenly ever since; many much needed population control reforms have come into being.

Before the advent of modern medicine, almost all serious birth anomalies (abnormalities) were not treatable. Those poor children who were born with such handicaps as microcephalus, hydrocephalus, myelomeningocele (spina bifida), heart defects, short bowel syndrome, and Down's syndrome (mongolism) could not be treated and therefore were not. Although surgical techniques have been developed which address most of these conditions, the wisdom of aggressive treatment in all cases remains questionable. Medicine can enable ex-utero fetuses to live with more serious conditions than earlier thought possible, but what right do doctors have to hand over children to mothers who might be overwhelmed at the prospect of caring for these children or committing them to institutional care? At first it was thought that the parents should, in the famous words of Drs. Raymond S. Duff and A.D.M. Campbell, have "much latitude" in making the decision whether their children should have aggressive care.[5] Then, grasping a more fundamental truth, doctors realized that they had to assume responsibility for conditions they were creating; it was their science after all that was imposing wildly handicapped children on parents so distraught, for obvious reasons, that they could not be expected to make rational decisions. In addition, the doctors were the only ones who could be expected to understand the complex problems these anomalies presented.

As this consensus emerged, Dr. Anthony Shaw, director of the Department of Pediatric Surgery at the City of Hope National Medical Center in California, came up with the first of the Quality of Life equations. His formula provided physicians with a guide to how they might treat a given ex-utero fetus with severe handicaps. The *quality* of the fetus's projected *life* was equivalent, he argued, to its *natural endowment*—both physical and intellectual—multiplied by the *support* the fetus was likely to receive from his *home* and *society*: $QL = NE \times (H + S)$. This formula was used as early as 1977 by the Oklahoma

Children's Medical Hospital in their efforts to advise parents what course of treatment should be pursued.[6]

Other such formulae, somewhat more sophisticated, were devised when physicians began to make the decision for parents. Since 1989, Bicksley's formula, $QL = NE \times S$, has become the standard guide.[7] The potential offspring's home is part of society after all, so that the variable $(H + S)$ in Shaw's formula was seen to include a redundancy. Some parents in the time since have demonstrated a pronounced dislike of this system. And who can blame them for feeling protective of their potential offspring? But the medical profession has decided it simply cannot shirk its responsibilities. Doctors alone know what heroic measures might be needed in each case, and only they know how much such care will drain from the limited health care resource (HCR). They alone, in other words, know at the outset what society, in their persons, is willing to devote to an ex-utero fetus. As a result of all this, the practice of infanticide or the newer and more appropriate term, *conservative management* (CM), has become widespread. One deleterious effect of this has been an escalation in medical costs, since doctors seem to want ever longer observation periods in which to make their decisions. Frankly, sometimes these periods extend far beyond the demands of prudence; such delays have even provoked charges of profiteering. Health care is an industry crying out for regulation.

Indeed, such regulation might help clear a path through the legal thicket woven by the introduction of once innovative techniques such as *in vitro* fertilization and embryonic transplants. As early as 1983 *Time* recognized that because of these procedures a "human being is literally conceived as a maufac-tured product, either as a flower of a growth indus-try, or, if a flaw appears, as industrial waste."[8] Soon afterward, in 1984, a case arose in which the frozen embryo of a couple who died in a plane crash provided a case in point of the legal ramifications of this concept. The couple had left an estate of some seven million dollars, and thus the question arose whether the embryo, being brought to term by a surrogate mother, might be the heir of this prop-erty.[9] The disposition of this case and others like it have only served to cancel each other out: no clear precedents have emerged. Yet the present adminis-tration has refused to coordinate CM by a regulatory body, professing abhorrence of the practice, and has actually done nothing through the attorney gen-eral's office but oppose such techniques as em-bryonic transfer when they have long since become accepted practices in society.

The practices of FTR and conservative manage-ment have produced a trade whose credit could well counterbalance that limited profiteering of which we spoke: the sale of fetal tissue. The trade in fetal tissue has grown from a one million dollar industry in 1984 to an estimated half billion dollar industry today.[10]

Such tissue has proven invaluable in the last fif-teen years to various medical research programs. The earliest programs to employ fetal tissue were generally devoted to ways of helping premature in-fants. The *International Life Times* for November 7, 1980, carried this report:

The U.S. Government has been funding some . . . experiments on live aborted babies

that are kept alive for the sole purpose of medical experimentation.

The live aborted babies were purchased from a Helsinki hospital with funds supplied by the U.S. Government . . . Finland had been selected for these experiments because of its extremely liberal abortion laws, which allow a physician to legally abort a fetus as old as five months.

Many of the unborn babies survive the abortion procedure.

The babies that survived were kept alive in an incubator in a Helsinki hospital and then were transported to Turku Hospital where the . . . experiments were conducted by Finnish researcher, Dr. Martti Kekomaki . . . [who] wrote: "They took the fetus and cut its belly open. They said they wanted the liver." Kekomaki added, "They carried the baby out of the incubator and it was still alive. It was a boy. It had a complete body, with hands, feet, mouth and ears. It was even secreting urine." The Finnish researcher conceded that the baby was not injected with an anesthetic when the doctor sliced open its stomach, but also maintained that this was of little concern to the experimenters, because, as he put it, "An aborted baby is just garbage." The baby would have had little chance of survival anyway, he contended . . . Explained Kekomaki, "We don't ask the mothers for their permission because, naturally, they would not allow it . . ."

Kekomaki stated that the purpose of his experiments is to find a way of feeding premature babies with brain nutrient. Con-

sequently, claims the Finnish researcher, he must chop off the heads of the babies to isolate the brain and process it into nutrients for food.

"We need the brains and livers of aborted fetuses if we are going to help premature babies," observed Kekomaki. "By feeding this special 'food' to them, their chances of health are much better."[11]

The extreme negative tone of the *International Life Times* (a rag of the now moribund antiabortion movement), although an obvious overreaction, reflected the uneasiness of many people when they first heard of these experiments. But thoughtful people eventually followed the line of argument first articulated by a doctor who was conducting experiments with live aborted fetuses at Cambridge. "We are simply using something," he said, "which is destined for the incinerator to the benefit of mankind. . . . Of course we would not dream of experimenting with a viable child. We would not consider that to be right."[12] The research has thus continued. *Heartbeat* magazine has reported progress on transplanting brain cells. These cells were also harvested from aborted babies.[13] Although the procedure has not been perfected, the knowledge gained has aided in other areas. Doctors in Southeast Asia, for instance, have made tremendous strides in studies on the effect of toxic gasses on Homo sapiens.[14] Much work has been done on chronic pain disorders which cannot be alleviated through drugs. For example, tic doloreaux (trigeminal neuralgia), in which violent and prolonged contractions cause the muscles at one side of the

Do we not marvel at the mother sparrow who, detecting the lameness of her newly hatched fledgling, shoves it from the nest? Is not the bird morally superior to the man stubbornly insisting upon protection for those whom nature has so clearly labeled "push me"?

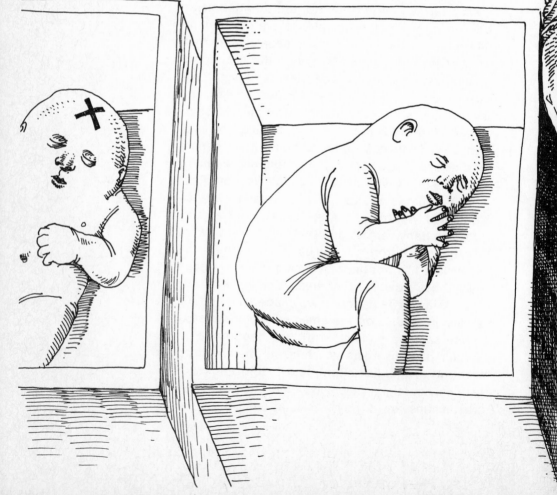

face to "seize up," has been found to be caused by the most obscure of viruses. We can now induce this syndrome in live aborted fetuses at will, and therefore may expect that immunology studies with targeted molecules will soon provide a remedy. We will also be able to use aborted fetuses in sophisticated testing procedures. (They have already been used in testing for thresholds of pain.)[15] Research with fetal embryos is also on the verge of discovering techniques whereby genetic information from a person afflicted with an illness attacking a vital organ can be isolated and nurtured toward the end of growing another organ, a heart or liver for example, which may then be transplanted into the victim's body.[16]

Fetal tissue, besides its role in these and other medical research programs, is now a valued source of collagen, which is used in cosmetics.[17] Fetal lymph glands are used in the manufacture of perfume, and, while this is discouraged in this country, many nations use fetal hides in making shoes. Indeed new uses are being found for this rich waste daily.

But again, because of a lack of regulation, much of the trade in fetal tissue is carried on in a somewhat underhanded way, being camouflaged by various "imaginative" means of accounting. Thus this source of commerce is lost to the tax base as a certified commodity.

In making population control measures a matter of national policy we may look for a model to the program of China, which has proven effective over the last decade. That China has been able to stabilize its population at nine hundred million is well known. How it has done so is not. The media have for inexplicable reasons been very conscientious about reporting the success of China's population control program but chary of going into the details of how this victory has been won. As of 1981, China had implemented its one-child incentive program.[18] Couples who contracted with the government to have one child were and are given preference in job advancements, salary increases, free education and health care for the child, extra ration coupons, and the largest housing units. In addition, the factories and offices and agricultural co-ops, which employ the mother and father directly, are urged by the government to sweeten this package with the addition of such benefits as an improved pension program. Couples who subsequently break this contract by having another child forfeit all these benefits and must refund the additional monies they have received, as any breach of contract carries with it certain penalties. If in the disastrous event a couple goes on to have a third child, the mother and father have their wages reduced by 10 percent and their career advancement necessarily suffers. The child, already guilty by proxy of its parents' overconsumption of the gene pool, is not allowed any ration coupons, and his entire family's food supply is, in fact, cut. The only real hindrance to the program has been the male chauvinism among the Chinese; they are prejudiced in favor of male babies and some would "keep trying" until they had a boy if the government did not intervene. Officials make every effort to reason with a profligate mother, sometimes speaking with her around the clock until she makes the appropriate decision.[19] It is true, as some have objected, that she can only make the right choice, and this smacks of coercion. But the American public is a long way from accepting such measures. We do need, though, to reconsider our position of viewing "family planning" exclusively as a matter of individual conscience, which allows us to multiply like rabbits if we so desire. We must come to see that society as a whole has a stake in each reproductive decision, and therefore must assume some responsibility for the decisions it would prefer its citizens to make.

More and more people are recognizing the virtue of the Chinese plan. The Soviet Union has copied it wholeheartedly to reduce its Asian and Moslem populations while encouraging the politically powerful Russians to gain in relative numbers. Although such population control measures can be used either generally—as the Chinese are doing— or selectively—as the Soviet Union has done—they are undoubtedly humankind's greatest hope at present for defusing the population bomb.

In regard to all of this, the United States has adopted the ostrich's posture of putting its head in the sand, although we have made indirect contributions for the last decade to China's birth-control program through our aid to the United Nations Fund for Population Activities.[20] These contributions throw our own policy in an even dimmer light when we consider the *prima facie* bad faith of encouraging heroic measures toward population control by others while refusing any sacrifice on our own part. The total picture, however, must finally be seen as simply chaotic since we have also gone ahead with our "humanitarian" relief efforts. An understanding of the role "triage" plays in medical ethics will show us our folly. During times of emergencies, according to triage theory, care ought to go neither to those for whom even heroic measures may not be adequate, nor to those who will get well anyway. It must be administered to those who present the severest cases in which there is still every hope of a cure. The principles of triage have long been accepted in battlefield hospitals and must now, given the exigencies of the time, be brought into our community facilities as well.

The supply of food stuffs and medical supplies given gratis to desolate portions of the earth, and the sale of wheat to those who can pay for it have won us, it must be admitted, friends in various nations. These countries tend to be paranoid about genocide, and have thus been encouraged in their own madness by our lunacy. Indeed, since our own population has for the most part stabilized due to what some economists call the "demographic transition"—and others plain glut and surfeit of riches—the righting of our reproductive behavior will serve as much or more as a good example than being of any immediate practical benefit to ourselves. (Businessmen should know, and many are recognizing, however, that population control will definitely improve our economy. That's already been admitted by the leading Fortune 500 companies, who have seen how China's system helps solve worker/management disputes, and tends to eliminate any resistance to the introduction of new technology.)

The world's poor in underdeveloped countries (UDCs) cannot be faulted for their untrammeled copulation. Who can begrudge them a moment of ecstasy in their numbingly routine lives? We must also consider that their own natural desires are reinforced by the sanctions of religions attuned to the adaptive needs of the species when mortality rates were astronomical. These beliefs have become vestigial, serving no good purpose at this time, but of course the local priests and shamans are more than reluctant to admit as much. If we cannot change our reproductive behavior in the full knowledge of why it would be prudent to do so, how can the average person in the UDCs be expected to go against everything in his being?

Therefore, Stage I of the new population control program must institute those measures the Chinese have adopted, with the exception, of course, of physical coercion. It must also include the following supplemental measures. 1) Sex education programs in the public schools and those mandated in private institutions should advance a new concept of "reproductive chastity," in which sexual pleasure of every kind is more than encouraged, but the state of being child-free as an adult is advanced as a high calling, equivalent in honor to the chastity of monks and the virginity of nuns in former days. Because mere sex education has not done the job—there being more teen-age pregnancies now than ever— extra-curricular clubs devoted to reproductive instruction should be encouraged as part of the total sex education package. At club meetings, after the sixth grade level, mature sex education counselors will be available to initiate their student-for-the-day into the mysteries of her or his orgasmic potential while, during each session, accustoming her or him to methods of contraception. 2) The signing of a one-child contract by a newly married couple should also include privileges along the lines of that wonderful old Hebrew custom exempting newly married men from service in the armed forces. Our contracts would exempt each spouse not only from the possibility of such duty but the very need to make a living. A $25,000 tax-free bonus grant on signing, adjusted upwards each year from the start of the plan for inflation, would effectively provide the couple with a year-long honeymoon. 3) In the event of a divorce each former spouse would still be obligated to refrain from procreating more than one child or he or she would have to repay one-half of those monies extended to the couple. 4) In the event of a third child being born to the couple, this breach of contract, in our more affluent society, would automatically lift two brackets the rate at which the couple's income would be assessed. In the event that a couple's income was already being assessed at the highest rate, a cash payment of 25 percent of the total value of their combined estate would be due to the Bureau of Population and Environment. The same dollar amount—*not* the same percentage of their already reduced estate—would have to be paid again for each additional child.

Further, I propose that the Bureau of Population and Environment regulate all conservative management decisions in neonatal wards. Bicksley's quality of life formula would guide all such decisions, and a code accounting for as many variables as possible in birth anomalies would fix the appropriate observation period for all treatment decisions. Birth certificates would not be issued to ex-utero fetuses until the regional ethics board decided whether or not the potential parents in question were to take the ex-utero fetus home and confer humanity upon it. Birth certificates would not be issued to conservative management candidates as that would necessitate formal burial arrangements.

The Bureau should also regulate all intra- and interstate traffic in fetal waste, which, as a certified commodity, would be called "homomass." The Food and Drug Administration and the other appropriate agencies would review potential uses of homomass, but the Bureau of Population and Environment would have the power of final review. Taxes collected by the Internal Revenue Service on the commodity homomass would be earmarked for use by the Bureau of Population and Environment.

With these measures in place we will alleviate much human suffering, both physical and emotional, and at the same time put society on a more equitable footing. On this basis, we can stride confidently toward other reforms, which will finally give each his due.

There may be some resistance, of course, to these measures. The frontier mentality, which expects that new lands, new opportunities, and new discoveries will magically solve whatever problems arise, is a deeply-ingrained part of the American character. However appealing such an attitude may be, it still flies in the face of the data calling for new managerial attitudes. So the "shakedown cruise" of Stage I may have its rough spots. But as the multitude of the plan's benefits follows, the wisdom of the majority will prevail, reducing the incidence of dissent. Almost everyone will soon look forward to our next measures with great eagerness and a sense of being part of a grand adventure.

The term "bureaucrat" may even gain in distinction.

In order to secure a just society we must come to terms with the underlying causes which create social inequities. The vicious cycle of population expansion, while it threatens the very life of the race, does afford us a view of these underlying causes which may prove our salvation. In population expansion we see the structure of civilization writ so large that its fault lines and fissures are apparent. This moment of crisis is also a moment of opportunity.

The problem, to state it once again, is that there are not enough resources to give each his due—much less his heart's desire. That problem has always been with us to some extent, however. It dates back to our prehistoric ancestors, the hominoids who began to organize their clans in the complex ways that allowed an animal with few gifts other than his intelligence to survive; stratagems that ultimately led to the creation of civilization. Long ago Darwin told us that every organism competes for its place in nature. The existence of each species has always been on the line, so to speak, because nature is more bountiful in creating new species than in providing for their welfare. She creates more demand than she is willing to satisfy. There exists, therefore, a "chronic labor surplus," with species vying for a seat in that economy.[1] Its balance depends on the dissonant harmony of one species devouring another or several others.

Humankind attempted to transcend this inherent conflict, first by the division of labor common to hunting and gathering peoples, and then by the creation of grain surpluses through settled agriculture. The formation of society, then, as the philosopher, Thomas Hobbes, showed, is first of all a transaction by which individuals trade absolute personal sovereignty for the security—the promise of abundant resources—possible within a group. These means of production did not, unfortunately, allow humankind to escape the dissonant harmony of nature but only transposed it into another key. Again, as Malthus showed, food production increases by simple addition while the populations it brings into being multiply geometrically. The success of society in producing goods has always been a source of its undoing as well. Any type of social organization—and this cuts right across every ideological line—can only maintain its own equilibrium by introducing its own brands of competitive elimination of the weak. The pressures on the resource base are "controlled" by the elimination of the poor, weak, and disabled through our four horsemen: famine, pollution, war, and death from disease and crime. Society has served the interests of its ruling classes well, but their security has always depended on a decidedly one-sided bargain, the virtual assent of the disfranchised to their exploitation. What we see in the population explosion is the outworking on a global scale of this guilty secret at the heart of every society.

Nature herself provides a means, however, for the preservation of an adequate number of species when cataclysmic pressures build up and threaten to destroy the entire system. In the last three decades, evolutionary theory has been undergoing crucial revision. The fossil record has been searched in vain for the "missing links" that would demonstrate the change of one species into another. What we have found are certain definite varieties during one epoch and completely different ones at another, with little or no transitional life forms between the two.[2] The record presents us with what has been called "punctuated equilibria"; that is, comparatively stable populations of life forms during a time when climatic and other conditions remain much the same,[3] whose stability is then upset by cataclysms, such as the impact of a meteor with the earth or the coming of an Ice Age. These cataclysms in turn precipitate "rapid speciation": those species which survive do so by making quantum leaps in design during relatively short periods of about fifty thousand years.

The metamorphosis of one species into an entirely new one occurs through the agency of cybernetics. Species cope with changing conditions through negative feedback and positive feedback. For example, let's examine the mechanism by which a cold-blooded snake controls his body temperature. Lying out on a rock in the sun, his body may become overheated. He then seeks to escape the positive stimulus of the sun by finding shade. When he has escaped the heat, he receives the negative feedback (the information) that the source of the heat is absent. Now see how a radical shift in his environment affects him. If his whole environment becomes too hot or too cold he continues to receive threatening messages; each positive feedback message amplifies the next, demanding that he must either become a warm-blooded creature or die.

The vicious cycle of the population explosion and the basic failure of civilization of which it speaks are the moral equivalent of the natural cataclysms which have always precipitated rapid speciation.[4] *We* must either reorganize our societal structures or die. This cannot be done merely by introducing the

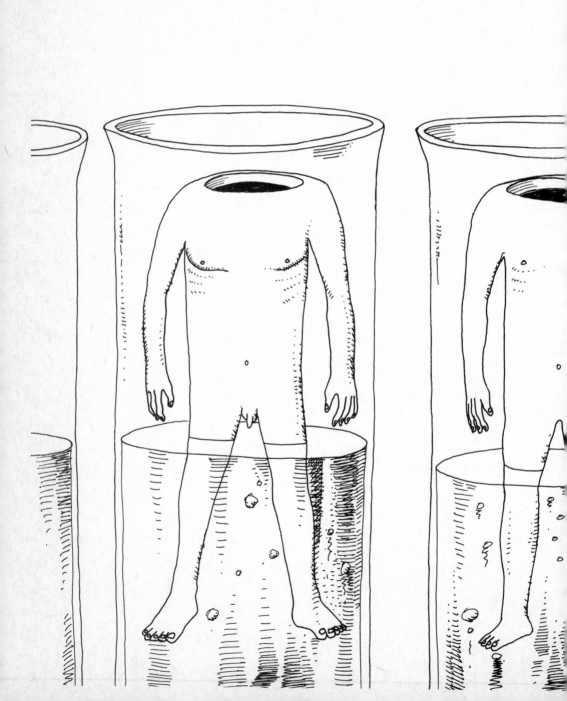

Would that medicine disassociate itself from metaphysics and join the 20th century. While the mills of Gary and Allentown gather dust, the application of Mr. Ford's genius conjures up a New Renaissance.

slight variations in cultural conditions humankind has looked to traditionally for the amelioration of our condition. As long as humankind retains its competitive nature, bred into it through the millennia, people will not cease competing against their fellow humans but will make every effort to "hotwire" the best of systems to their own advantage. Humankind itself must be changed. And quickly. Human beings must become super-rational creatures capable of making those sacrifices for the good of society which their own happiness requires and social justice demands.

Fortunately, just within the last half of this century, humankind has acquired the knowledge to extend consciously nature's own mode of adaptation in times of crisis: we have unlocked the secrets of the genetic code (DNA) and have learned how to manipulate it to our advantage. Genetic surgical techniques are on the verge of eliminating Down's syndrome, sickle cell anemia, and other congenital (that word will be gladly forgotten!) conditions. Each newborn now has its memory improved as much as 35 percent with the introduction of KP35 during the third month of his gestation period. Many other such life-long enhancements of genetic endowment are on the way.[5]

We are close to the time when we can purposefully carry out our own rapid speciation. What a triumph that will be: the theme of scientific papers, the topic of every politician's thankful address, and the subject of euphoric media presentations. The ages have all testified that humankind's role in the universe is to bring Nature to self-awareness. Our ancestors could hardly have known how true that is going to be! For we are now on the way to replicating Nature's very methods in becoming, truly, the authors of our own destiny—the gods of our world. Nature herself will have to bow to the profusion of useful plant and animal species we will make out of the information stored in the genetic codes (or species) that now exist. For we will not need to duplicate what was necessary to blind force and random chance; we may create a *new economy of existence* that is not based on competition for scarce resources but of ready sharing. What is misbegotten in the world around us will be re-created, what of value cherished, what of potential fulfilled!

Despite the power available to us in our new understanding and use of genetics, our task of creating the world anew from ground zero will not be an easy one. The task of negotiating the priority of competing interests in our society will be particularly difficult, as I shall discuss presently. What is perhaps most daunting about this task is that the wisdom of the ages has nothing to tell us about how to conduct these negotiations.[6] Prophets and seers in their spiritual ecstasies may have envisioned such a time, but it remained absolutely hidden to them beyond the walls of a heavenly city or a "happily-ever-after" state, the most common metaphors for the end of their knowledge.

As Mr. William B. Provine, in a study guide designed to accompany a PBS TV series entitled, "Hard Choices," writes:

The new eugenics will force some very difficult choices between individual freedom and public welfare and, as I argue elsewhere, we have to look to ourselves as human beings to

write the moral rules that will govern these choices.[7]

"Look to ourselves as human beings." What a fine phrase! Indeed, what else could we look to ourselves as?

The idea of humankind being its own god is an ancient dream; perhaps more than anything else it unites us with those hominoids who first organized proto-societies. While simply an extrapolation of our primal impulse toward securing our survival, it has nevertheless not always been looked upon favorably, at least in theory. The Bureau of Population and Environment would definitely have a titanic public relations problem if it advanced this notion baldly. The human imagination rebels at recognizing its ties to the animal world through evolution. It does not want to remember the insecurity of its ape-like ancestors, the primal fear that gave rise to civilization. Therefore, in its bad faith, it refuses to acknowledge the sweep of its most basic ambition: to sever its ties to the animal world forever by remaking itself into the image of a self-sufficient being. Stage II of my proposal thus calls for various measures that will change that imagination. We must begin by recognizing our natural allies in this endeavor and proceed with specific recommendations that will bring our mutual goal into view. Once humanity glimpses that nothing stands in the way of its ultimate ambition, it will not, I feel sure, be content with anything less.

The proper reform of our collective imagination mandates that we inculcate in the public an understanding of the philosophic implications of bioengineering. Indeed the notion that existence precedes essence or, another way of putting it, that form follows function, must become as familiar to the populace as advertising jingles. (We should in fact make a TV campaign integral to our educational efforts.) Through bioengineering, form will follow function because the decision of what kind of creatures and human beings we create (the form of these things) will depend on what kinds of jobs and tasks we want them to perform (the function of these things). Our decisions about the tasks we want to get done will be determined prior to the creation of life forms that will perform these tasks. When the techniques of bioengineering are fully perfected, nothing can be said to follow as a "natural" outcome of its design. In designing nature ourselves, we will of necessity arbitrate the specific ends or purposes of all we create. Thus, again, the forms of things will flow from these decisions, from what we will first determine to be their functions.

But how shall we decide what ends to pursue? what tasks ought to be accomplished? what creatures to create? The great tribunal today is science.[1] East and West differ on nearly every matter of political import, but they both share the scientific method. They both submit themselves to its judgment. For when the truth can be demonstrated, as in one group of scientists repeating the experiments of another, then all have a stake in unanimity. Anything else is simply willful ignorance. And as this deprives its adherents of the power that would be theirs otherwise, the foolishness of this course is evident. For this reason, as Edward O. Wilson said in his landmark book, *Sociobiology: The New Synthesis* (Harvard, 1975), "ethics [must be] removed from the hands of the philosophers and 'biologicized' . . ."[2] Only science is capable of unifying our efforts; thus, only science will prove a sure guide in ranking competing values. Science must dictate what our new ethical system shall be.

In order to "biologicize" ethics we will have to address the primary sources of ethics and transform the institutions which pass on these codes. Religion and its expression in various churches, especially those of the Judeo-Christian tradition, must be the first focus of our attention. The Western tradition of the liberal arts and its dissemination through educational institutions must be the second.

Religion. Sadly, as we have seen, humankind's greatest prophets never contemplated the technological context in which we live, and thus their words have little applicability today. Worse, they often stand in foursquare opposition to even thinking about the course global problems and our technology dictate. Indeed, the struggle to empty the collective mind of the religious imagination will be of the utmost concern. We may see the reasons for this difficulty by comparing the basic outlook of the scientific mind—which alone is suited to chart our course for the future—and the religious mind.

According to the religious view, humankind enjoys a special place in the pattern of things. Just what that special place might be varies from one religion to another. We may say with some degree of accuracy, however, that it was generally supposed that we had a unique relation as a species with the gods, or God, either by virtue of being more like them than animals are, or of being loved by the gods, or of sharing their intelligence. In the Judeo-Christian view, the dominant tradition in the Old and New Worlds, "man" was said to be "created in the image of God." (We may see, in passing, something of the primitive nature of this view in the very designation of our species as *man*. The term recalls epochs when it was felt that women did not fully share the quality of "humanness" with men and hence were excluded by the very word which referred to the species from the rights and privileges due it.) The idea is that there is some divinity which crowns us. Our form, then, precedes our function; we act the way we do, we have the freedoms and responsibilities we do, because we were made or designed in a certain way, in the image of God. If this were true, we would be treading on perilous ground by tinkering with that design.

Science finds this impossible to accept because it cannot determine what it means. As positivism has shown, statements that cannot be empirically verified, such as "man is made in the image of God," are simply meaningless.[3] To demonstrate the reasoning behind this, let's compare one of Piero della Francesca's paintings of the "Annunciation" with a blown-up photo of a computer chip.[4] Piero della Francesca's painting has a stately symmetry which appeals to us. It may appeal to us immensely. But when we try to say why we like it, we are reduced to acknowledging that "there's no accounting for taste." We cannot demonstrate anything about what makes the painting a good painting *empirically,* apart from certifying the materials of which it is made. The only meaningful thing to say about it is a statement which represents how it makes us feel. Such a statement cannot obligate another person to feel the same way, and thus the "truth" of what makes it a good painting must remain private.

In the same way, the statement, "man is made in the image of God," has only a subjective meaning. It makes people feel good, bad, or indifferent. But we cannot demonstrate the objective truth of the statement in any way that another person can verify. Thus, the only "truth value" of such a statement lies in its emotional value for whoever speaks it. Since its truth value cannot be demonstrated or shared, it has no exact meaning, and thus it can hardly be an operational definition for our purposes. Theology begins with such objectively meaningless statements and proceeds to add one on top of another until the most magnificent cathedrals of thought have been constructed out of absolutely nothing.

On the other hand, we may make many statements about the blow-up of the computer chip about which anyone can determine the veracity. If we say that it is made of silicon, that it was made by a third generation accelerator, that it was made to work in a 256 bit computer, all of these statements can be verified by independent testing. So we see that science, in that its knowledge can be shared, brings us together, while religion divides us. A Hindu, a Jew, and a fundamentalist Christian will agree with the nonsectarian scientist that the earth rotates once on its axis every twenty-four hours, or that the half-life of U235 is 7.1×10^8 years. This is data, not dogma. And it is to this realm we must turn for guidance.

While we must make every attempt to preserve religion as an anthropological study, an artifact produced in the early history of the race, we must eventually phase it out of American society. There are historic precedents for this: necromancy, astrology, and alchemy have all been phased out of human affairs as science made its way along. This cannot be done by fiat, of course. It will take time. I propose, therefore, that in the immediate future we take a two-pronged approach to religion. Along one prong of the fork, religion, as it already has been to a great extent, will be phased out of the decision-making

Though the statisticians lead us to believe religion plays so vital a role in everyday life, one is left to wonder why the gold paved dreamscape of Television Land should so fittingly convey the gospel to the masses... from one fantasy to another no doubt.

process. Along the other, we shall encourage—at least for a time—certain benign types of popular religion.

The first prong. Screening procedures can be set up, such as we now have for juries, to ensure that government officials will not attempt to bash in the Jeffersonian wall of separation between church and state. Precedent for screening like this may also be found in our present policies for military conscription: pacifists who would not obey an order to fire are not acceptable, although they make fine citizens and may expect the government to protect all their rights under the law. In all of these cases, prior attitudes that will compromise the process in question rule out a person's participating. It is reasonable, then, for society to establish religious neutrality as a minimum requirement for all who participate in running the country. If at every juncture we had someone who was confused as to the form/function distinction, someone who believed that essence precedes existence, then it would be impossible to attend to the welfare of the species.

To take religion away from the general population immediately would be a grave error, however. Marx himself said that religion was the opiate of the people. Yet Lenin, Stalin, and their successors have all made the mistake of seriously underestimating the addiction of their people to this narcotic. Direct pressures exerted to deprive the people of their dope have been counterproductive. The greatest source of resistance to the ambitious experiment in cultural adaptation in the Soviet Union has been the Russian Orthodox church. Hungary, Czechoslovakia, Poland, Yugoslavia, Bulgaria, and now in 1992 even *Albania*

have all been pitched into social upheaval by anar-
chistic elements that have had close ties with the
Catholic and Orthodox churches. In the last decade,
Latin America has become an international powder
keg because of theology. Resistance is widespread
even among the Chinese to the extermination there
of the wholly foreign Judeo-Christian tradition.

Stalin did learn his lesson, however, and we
should take our cues from his example. When the
Nazis were about to destroy Mother Russia in World
War II, Stalin appealed to his people on the basis of
their cultural tradition to fight for their country; he
allowed his people to practice their religion openly
for the first time since 1918.[5] Only the love of God
proved strong enough to repulse the Nazis' attack.
That love, so strong, so determined, so irrational,
must be steered into appropriate channels, as Stalin's actions show us. Popular piety in fact can accomplish the nearly impossible in keeping citizens
humble and about their tasks. It makes them decent,
orderly, hard working, meek, clean, helpful, cheerful, and above all, loyal. It should be encouraged as
long as it provides an outlet for whatever frustra-
tions people may feel as the awkward first stages of
society's reform begin. Encouraging religious expression in churches makes the work done in imagination reform by the first prong appear minimal.
But its full significance will only be known later, after
public life has been free of religious influence for a
certain amount of time.

The second prong, then. Government funding
should be given to television evangelists, since the
service they perform in diverting the attention of
millions of people is actually a public service. There

should be federal grants for the printing and distribution of books and leaflets on prayer, Bible study, and long-range prophecy. (Curbs would have to be placed on studies in short-term prophecy since this rouses people to scrutinize current events for signs of "the end.") Federal funding for religious activities in mass media affords an additional bonus to the good of encouraging middle-class values: what the government supports financially it can regulate. Obviously federal funding must go only to evangelists who will honor the constitutional principle of church/state separation. Those who violated the Constitution here would, of course, have their licenses revoked. We could be sure to snare such obstreperous characters as Dr. Jerry Falwell in this way.

Though rather dimwitted, the Dr. Falwells of this world are a real threat to social progress. They are seemingly incapable of understanding the form/function distinction aright. Indeed, as much as we would regret having to take summary actions toward such groups, the combination of irrational values with the unthinking commitment that they exhibit may doom any attempt at dialogue. As Daniel C. Maguire in *The New Subversives* has observed:

> **The biblical fundamentalists, to put it mildly, do not enter debate with respect for their opponents. Those who oppose them are either insane or immoral. Herein is a major problem that arises with the entrance of the deviant fundamentalists into the political process in a big and organized way. Political discourse in a democracy necessitates a modicum of respect**

operating among the participants. The alternative to this is the fascist solution, which bans opposing views. That is not the American way. It *is* the way of the New Right. Censorship is their natural reflex. . . .

The New Rightists come to us with smiles and unctuous righteousness, hiding their mean purposes under biblical and patriotic guises . . . the reality they represent must be faced and called to task. These people are not simply one more fair-minded interest group making its way in the world of politics. They are subversives. Their programs offend both religion and the cause of political peace and justice.[6]

Forward looking groups have long ago recognized this, so that we do, thankfully, have real allies in discounting the presumptions of the many stump preachers and their Catholic cousins. Even people among their own ranks recognize their manifest faults. The Secretary of the evangelical Wayfarers Society said in 1987, "Dr. Jerry [Falwell] and Brother Pat [Robertson] are an embarrassment to the church. They preach a new kind of polyethism: Polly Glot, Polly Ester, and Polly Anna. I'd like to think I have more in common with a fair-minded liberal."[7] And Mary Daly, a Roman Catholic theologian, has shown the absurdity of that body's own confession in light of today's agenda.

I propose that another form of reversal has been the idea of redemptive incarnation uniquely in the form of a male savior. . . . A patriarchal divinity of his son is exactly *not* in a position to save us from the horrors of a pa-

triarchal world. Does this mean, then, that the women's movement points to, seeks, or in some way constitutes a *rival* to "the Christ"? . . . In its depth, because it contains a dynamic that drives beyond Christolatry, the women's movement *does* point to, seek, and constitute the primordial, always present, and future Antichrist. . . . I suggest that the mechanism of reversal has been at the root of the idea that the "Antichrist" must be something "evil." What if this is not the case at all? What if the idea has arisen out of the male's unconscious dread that women will rise up and assert the power robbed from us? . . . Seen from this perspective, the Antichrist and the Second Coming of *women* are synonymous. . . . There is a bond, then, between the significance of the women's revolution as Antichrist and its import as Antichurch. Seen in the positive perspective in which I have presented it, as a spiritual uprising that can bring us beyond sexist myths, the Antichrist has a natural correlative in the coming of the Antichurch, which is a communal uprising against the social extensions of the male Incarnation myth, as this has been objectified in the structures of political power.[8]

Clearly any hope that my proposal will be able to move forward toward its goal of a just, free, and humane society for all persons must presuppose the removal of these obstacles of reactionism and dogmatism. As Ms. Daly's remarks show, thoughtful people, such as those in the women's movements, the gay liberation movement, and related causes, have long understood that the forces of obstruction and obscurantism are indeed what they have claimed to be all along, namely *Christ*-ian.

Merely eliminating the fulminations of the Dr. Falwells from our mass media will not be enough. Religious people must come to see that the tax exempt status of their institutions amounts to a government subsidy of their activities. The state thus has a right to insure that churches on the local level are not being used as fronts for political activities, which would be another violation of that wall of separation and a threat to government regulation of campaign funding.[9] In this regard, the government has an overriding interest in maintaining the integrity of its system, to the point that it cannot be content with putting out the brush fires of political activism after they get started. A review board, consisting in equal parts of members of the judiciary and clergy associated with the National Council of Churches, must therefore decide the acceptability of those men and women coming out of the seminaries which all churches and their denominations wish to ordain. As the state now insists on granting its own marriage licenses, so it must begin accepting its responsibilities in licensing the clergy. The guiding principle of the review board has already been articulated by Hans Kung. This eminent Roman Catholic theologian has stated that reconciliation and everyday service to our fellow man have priority over service to God.

Indeed the review board must see to it that all clergy are possessed of the enlightened opinions that have come down to the churches through what is known, I believe, as higher criticism. During the period in which we wish to encourage benign forms of piety, clergypersons must *not* announce the truths higher criticism imparts: that the supernatural element in Christianity is simply untrue. The clergy must lead their flocks along to the greener pastures of a demythologized faith through *using* the old words and phrases and then glossing these with purely naturalistic explanations. In this way they will be able to insinuate at every turn the cold hard truth of their disbelief, which their congregations might not be willing to tolerate right off. This course has been pursued to great effect already in the mainline Protestant denominations, providing much more comfortable seating to the dozens who keep showing up in every church on a Sunday morning. It remains to be introduced in parishes kept in the darkness of the old superstitions—those which present the most unseemly tableau of kneeling figures with fervent prayers and spittle on their lips.

At the end of the period in which the populace has been allowed to keep at its ethno-religious knitting, the central intelligence of the review boards, the Council For Ultimate Concerns, will call a national ecclesiastical conclave. All licensed clergy—that is, all clergy—will be required to attend. Those rational enough to see the superfluous nature of regimented invocation of a nonexistent deity, or, as it is sometimes called, prayer, will put forward the proposition that the use of all churches be amended as follows: acknowledging the great value of those buildings and other properties held by various churches, they will suggest that they be dedicated to more essential uses, turned into museums and community recreation centers. No attempt will be made by the government to force abolition of traditionalist activities. National conclaves will simply be called until the motion passes. Each clergyperson will then be charged with the task of persuading those die-hard souls who have kept attending meaningless services that their religious duty demands one last sacrifice: that they turn the deeds of their churches over to the state.

Education. In our attempts to change the collective imagination of our people, the schools are the last crucial battleground. In other less-developed societies, the home will have to be obliterated as a transmitter of worn-out values. But, with the development in our society of universal divorce, single-parent households in which the parent works full-time, and no-parent households, and the establishment of teenage rebellion as a rite of passage for all, we may discount the home as an influence of any importance in modern American life. Indeed, as early as the Carter administration, the American Home Economics Association, in relation to the President's White House Conference on Families, drafted what was at the time a far-sighted new definition of the family: "Two or more persons who share resources, share responsibilities for decisions, share values and goals, and have a commitment to one another over time . . . regardless of blood, legal ties, adoption, or marriage."[10] This would have been so vague as to be meaningless, if not for its landmark status in the history of consciousness raising. It marked the time when "the family" had become nothing but a blank space, which invited other influences to fill its traditional role. Day-care and the schools have invaded this empty territory, and as a result are now more important than ever.

There has already been much progress in education to prepare the next generation for the changes it will see in its lifetime. Textbooks have been purged so that no child will ever encounter a female engaging in a stereotypical activity such as cooking. And all superstitious notions such as a Prime Mover setting the evolutionary process going and directing its progress have been ruled out of the classroom as unscientific by law.

Two changes, one minor, the other major, are still needed. Sex education programs, the minor concern, do not always present every alternative lifestyle in a favorable light. The efforts of the Task Force on Child-Adult Relations have been directed toward righting this wrong. They have proposed "to improve the public image of pedophiles" through:

a. **Oversight of sex education and psychology curricula in public schools, colleges, and universities, seeking to eliminate old stereotypes and falsehoods regarding pedophilia [sex between adults and children] and children's sexuality.**

b. **Consultations with authorities on mental health and human sexual behavior to encourage a humane attitude toward pedophilia.**

c. **Legislative lobbying to reduce legal sanctions against pedophile behavior in particular and all consensual sexual behavior in general, and to increase children's rights to self-determination.**

d. **Liaison with feminist and other groups to establish the principle that the goals of all liberation groups are essentially the same: the**

**elimination of sexist, authoritarian regimenta-
tion of human lives, and that the liberation of
children is the *sine qua non* of all human liberation.**[11]

The Task Force also proposes to publish and dis-
tribute "literature to increase public awareness of
children's sexual and emotional needs, especially in
the light of research and cognitive development."[12]
In this connection, Andre Lord, speaking to the National Third World Lesbian and Gay Conference in
Washington, D.C as long ago as 1979, made the following observation:

**They [children] have a right to grow, free from
diseases of racism, sexism, classism, homophobia, and the terror of any difference. The
children will take what we do and carry it on
through their visions, and their visions will be
different from ours. But they need us as role-
models, to know that they are not alone in
daring to define themselves outside the ap-
proved structures. They need to know our triumphs and errors.**[13]

One of these errors, we may say with no conde-
scension to Mr. Lord, has been to exclude pedosadism from the province of our compassion. Dick
Tinney, author of *Brandish The Rod* and the leading
proponent of pedosadism, has said, "Every parent
has seen children hitting and kicking each other 'for
no reason.' We have been terribly reluctant to view
this behavior as essentially sexual; but I have found
that every child once he has found gratification for
these displaced sexual overtures in a healthy beating becomes docile and content."[14]

The efforts of these individuals and their associates are terribly important, not only for their explicit ends, but also for the acceptance of the right view of function and form, existence and essence. Gays, and others who live out alternative lifestyles, have led the way in showing us what it means to be self-created. They have seen that there is nothing "natural" about "human nature." That once we truly give up the notion that "God" created us with his own ends in mind, which are made evident by how we are made, then we can remake our lives and finally ourselves to suit without hesitation our own purposes. Alternative lifestyles have done yeoman's work in preparing the ground for alternative life forms.

The full acceptance of alternative lifestyles in sex education curricula is at hand, of course, and little change will be needed in this regard; so it is the minor concern here. The major concern will be a new and philosophically consistent attitude toward the teaching of the humanities. Mr. Edward Wilson, who voiced the need to "biologicize" ethics, has also commented that: "We may find that there is an overestimation of our deepest yearnings."[15] Regrettably we must blame the poets of times past for this. Their sins were not of commission, of course—they could not have known what they were doing. But the effect of all of literature, as well as the traditional understanding of the other "humanities," has been to foist on humankind the view that suffering may lead to transcendence. Homer's Odysseus is presented as if all his sufferings make him into a better man. In reality, the story must have come out of the experience of a particularly bad sailor, who probably suffered from schizophrenic delusions. In the same way, Shakespeare's Hamlet has forever been hailed as a tragic figure. But what is tragedy? It is a compound of chance and meaningless violence. Hamlet suffers obviously from an Oedipal complex. In Shakespeare's day, we realize all too well, there was nothing to do about this but wax eloquent. But we can take our contemporary Hamlets to a psychotherapist who will heal them. Again, people have derived an experience of "transcendence" from Shakespeare's *King Lear,* a victory of the human spirit through suffering. But what do we have here? The whole play is based on the once fond but now irrelevant notions of family loyalty and honor. We live in an age which has seen through the illusion of transcendence and its supernatural trappings. It is an age in which we have experienced the "triumph of the therapeutic"—which will be infinitely more triumphant with the full use of bioengineering at our disposal. And what are we to make of Dante except that he turned the factual reality of the stimulus-response basis of behavior into the most complicated sublimation of negative (hell) and positive (heaven) reinforcement.

It's true that most modern and contemporary poets have accepted our demythologized world, but they have shamelessly—because they knew they were doing it—turned their own egotistical, masturbatory fantasies into false simulacra of life, distorting mirrors which have hidden far more than they have revealed. Many of these poets have committed suicide, and for very good reasons. If we had had a cure for their conditions, their need to write as well as their illnesses, we can be sure, would have disappeared overnight. The only justification anyone has had in the last fifty years for studying literature has

been purely hedonistic. We can understand the pleasures of reading. But those pleasures are far outweighed by the mistaken and disastrous coddling of people's yearnings, which literature brings with it. As Plato showed in his *Republic,* a utopian vision of a very early date, the poets can have an absolutely subversive influence.

Banning literature alone from our schools will not do the job. The plastic arts and music are nothing but yearning. The study of history, except as those quantitative scientists of history now practice it, is shot through with yearning. No. Every branch of the humanities must be scientized, as in the case of history, or banned outright. We must even be careful in anthropology not to mislead our students into thinking that the correlatives of ancient societies to our own arts and humanities have any justification. Anthropology must be artifacts for artifacts' sake. It must conform much more closely to the standards set by sociology, in which there rarely has been a trace of anything like yearning. This measure cannot be urged with too much vigor. When I think of the hopes that have been inspired in me by literature! The beliefs I have had to sever one by one in my own torturous, prolonged, agonizing process of self-authentication . . . well, enough of this.

In addition to religion and education, one other possible focus of attention comes to mind: mass media, particularly television. It will be admitted that movies and dramatic television programs do give some aid and comfort to irrational yearnings. In general, however, they are far more realistic than literature. They do not arouse much more than the desire for sex. Television, in the most positive way, stifles any attempt at thinking along any other lines.

And the contribution its news programs make to our agenda can hardly be reckoned. We may, therefore, simply praise the mass media and pass on.

With religious belief expunged from our minds, the church converted to better uses, sex education reformed, and the study of the humanities and art banned, the public's imagination will be ready for those ambitious reforms I shall propose shortly. All that remains in Stage II is to ratify what we have done thus far by issuing an identity card, as they have in China, to each citizen during Universal Citizenship Examination week. The cards will be given out at every polling place in the country so that a record of the entire citizenry can be processed and entered into the data bank of a federal computer. We will be able to check on the success of our efforts by asking two questions of each potential citizen: 1) Do you believe that a human being only becomes a human being when she or he has the ability to interact with our culture? And, 2) Do you believe in any gods or God? Following the replies of "yes" and "no" respectively the potential person will be declared a citizen.[16] Those who fail this most simple of all tests will have one week to review the booklet, "Entering the Future: Humanity's Ultimate Destiny." Any subsequent failure will demand that the person take time out in a suitable setting—as many V.A. psychiatric hospitals will be converted for this use as necessary—to consider the ease of saying, first, "yes," and then, "no." Those who cannot accomplish such a simple task will, unhappily, demonstrate that they do not have the ability to interact with their culture and are therefore subhuman. Provision will be made for them in Stage III.

The measures my proposal has contemplated thus far in Stages I and II have been, respectively, remedial and preparatory. Stage III will implement truly positive reforms at last. With its collective imagination reformed, the public will receive the glad tidings that Stage III has begun with once unimaginable additions having been made to the Bill of Rights. The old document will be amended to include these provisions: 1) Each citizen shall have access to a plentiful supply of *clean* water. 2) Each citizen shall have a right to a balanced diet regardless of socio-economic standing. 3) Enough wilderness will be preserved for each citizen to be allotted a share of land where he may look to a horizon bare of any sign of civilization. (To be known in the shorthand of common parlance as the Right of Solitude.) 4) Each citizen shall be given access without any charge to educational resources for as long as she or he desires. 5) Each citizen shall have guaranteed employment in whatever field she or he chooses. 6) Each citizen shall be given a fair share of the "information wealth" of the nation by being connected through a home computer (a gift from the government) to the files of the Library of Congress. 7) Each will have a right to unlimited sexual gratification in whatever mode she or he chooses. The government will announce that in the rest of Stage III it will do everything possible to confer these new rights on each citizen.

One or two of these provisions may appear impossible to enforce, but nothing will be impossible any longer, remember, to a race that will soon be able to control its destiny absolutely. The new amendments will demand further tinkering with our population control methods, however. It must be admitted that the noncoercive reforms of Stage I were, in fact, coercive in a limited sense. What would a formerly wealthy couple with six children (the last four excess) who had had all their worldly possessions stripped from them do?

Compassion demands that we keep people from making such disastrous choices. Therefore, five years from the date of the Universal Citizenship Examination a Population Census will be taken. Every adult and all children shall appear at their neighborhood polling place. Children, teenagers, and adults who have not yet procreated will be given new day-glo orange identity cards with two white circles stippled on them. After any birth in which a citizen is an agent, one of the white circles on his card will be punched out. (Those adults who have been agents in one birth already will be given orange cards with one stipple punched and the other intact.) When both stipples have been punched the agent will be given a black card, obliging him to appear at a federally operated birth control counseling center where she or he will be sterilized. Persons who have already been an agent in the birth of two or more offspring at the time of the Population Census will be given these black cards as well, with the same instructions, except in the case of a woman presently carrying her third fetus or more; she will be given a blue card that will oblige her to undergo an FTR procedure. All third and subsequent children born to a couple constitute, as our penal taxes will have indicated, an excess allotment of the gene pool; these excess children will be given fire-engine red cards, whatever their ages, and will be instructed to report to the counseling centers for sterilization as well. The new rights will then be conferred on everyone holding an identity card.[1]

The cases of those who are not able because of physical or mental impairment to present themselves at their polling places will be reviewed by the newly constituted Cut-off Point Impairment (CPI) Office of the Bureau of Population and Environment. Those who have already been administering the QL equation in cases of birth anomalies should be appointed to head this branch office, as its functions will simply extend the logic of the QL formula.

It will be the Bureau's expressed desire to extend the new rights to every citizen. Those who, by virtue of physical or mental impairment, frustrate that desire cannot, sadly, be citizens in the full sense. Mercy demands that a corollary right be derived from the new rights; just as the implicit "right of privacy" was derived from the explicit rights stated in the old Bill, and then used so effectively to justify FTR-on-demand, so the right not to endure unnecessary suffering, the right not to exist, may be presented with equal logic as the corollary of the Right to Solitude. After all, it is a logical impossibility to grant rights to noncitizens, to confer human privileges on sub-humans; and we may in turn determine who is sub-human by whether it is possible to confer rights upon them. Can someone in a vegetative coma take her or his place in the universal work force? Can a senile old woman enjoy educational opportunities? To be outside the pale of these liberating rights shows us that someone is enduring a life of such pain or unawareness that it is not worthy to be lived. Life is a heavy encumbrance for these poor souls, which we must, if there is any decency in us, help them put off.

The CPI office will therefore come up with a Table

of Acceptability Components. This, with the aid of computers, will be drawn up with encyclopedic inclusiveness, but the above rubrics should guide its efforts. Perhaps the following short list of conditions, which would certify a case as not acceptable, will also help us to envision the work of the CPI office. Senility, Parkinson's disease, retardation, incontinence, insanity, epilepsy, para- and quadraplegia, multiple sclerosis, spinal meningitis, Alzheimer's disease, AIDS, sickle cell anemia, Tay-Sachs disease, muscular dystrophy, cancer of any type other than surface skin malignancies, advanced heart disease, chronic criminal behavior, chronic depression, chronic poverty, and chronic podiatric ills—all of these will surely disqualify any ex-utero fetus, however advanced in age, from full humanhood. More poor people will be able to enjoy the rights of citizenship than we may imagine at first glance; many have desirable traits—smooth skins, liquid eyes, good singing voices, athletic skills, rhythm—that should remain in the gene pool.

Thus as we move toward becoming a super-race, there will be a gradual winnowing of tragic affliction from our numbers. Our mean intelligence will be higher through the elimination of retardation. Money will be more plentiful since there will be fewer sharing it. Pathetic scenes of penury will be seen no more. Gone from state institutions will be those human vegetables who don't know if it is night or day. Gone from federal prisons will be psychotic mass murderers waiting for society to end its heartlessly protracted deliberations on the death penalty. Gone from the ghetto streets will be the spindly children trying to cool their asphalt-burned feet in the hydrant water that splashes along the gutter. The oppression and injustice that have obliged these elements to bear the burden of existence will be no more. No more illegal aliens will deny proper citizens their jobs. No more black teenage mothers—children themselves—will be added in perpetuity to our welfare rolls. Gone, in fact, will be the welfare rolls, the whole kit 'n caboodle. There will be no more crime, no more poverty. The continuing population will be affluent, intelligent, articulate, civil, attractive, aware, and productive. Everyone will seem upwardly mobile, although, strictly speaking, the predicaments that usually prompted the ambitious to rise in the world will be gone, and therefore no such metaphoric direction as "up" shall exist.

The CPI office, by necessity, will also administer the Positive Ending and Disposal Program (PEAD). The program's name comes from the writing of that pioneer in the neoeugenics field, Joseph Fletcher. In an article in *The American Journal of Nursing,* Dr. Fletcher, nearly twenty years ago in 1973, insinuated the principles underlying the CPI office and PEAD.

It is ridiculous to give ethical approval to the positive ending of subhuman life in utero as we do in therapeutic abortions for reasons of mercy and compassion, but refuse to approve of positively ending a subhuman life in extremis. If we are obliged to put an end to a pregnancy when an amniocentesis reveals a terribly defective fetus, we are equally obliged to put an end to a patient's hopeless misery. . . .[2]

The pavilion at the new headquarters of the Bureau

As the enlightened Governor Richard Lamm so aptly reminded our aged back in 1984 "you've got a duty to die and get out of the way. Let the other society, our kids, build a reasonable life."

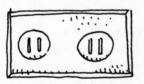

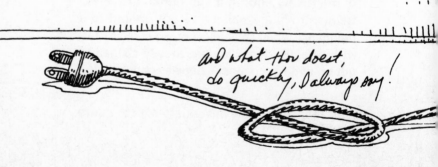

and what thou doest, do quickly, I always say!

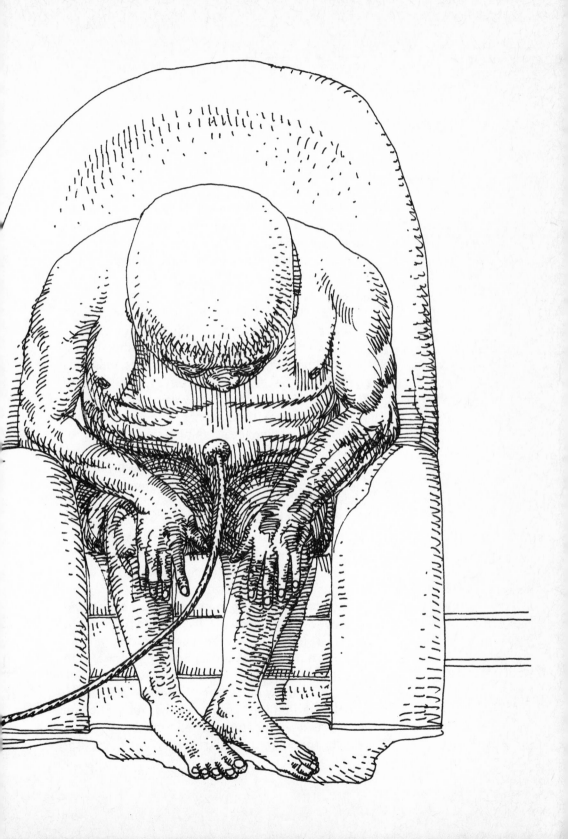

of Population and Environment, which shall house the CPI office, will be named the Joseph Fletcher Pavilion in honor of this man and his invincible ideals. The very term *PEAD* owes itself to Dr. Fletcher, as we see in the above quote, who hit upon the phrase "positively ending" as a scientific alternative to the traditionalist "kill." Joseph Fletcher might be said to be the "patron saint" of the population planning and eugenics movement.

PEAD will be administered in two places, with means appropriate to each. Those candidates for positive endings (PEs) in hospitals and other institutions will be treated where they are. This will, once again, hardly be novel. In the April 11, 1983, issue of *Time* magazine, the question was asked: "Is denying food and water to a patient of any age the logical extension of ending life sustaining treatment?" Prudent members of the legal profession promptly answered, yes. University of Texas Law Professor, John Robertson, addressed this question in an American Civil Liberties Union handbook, entitled *The Rights of the Critically Ill.* " 'If you can legally and ethically take a respirator from a patient, then the decision has already been made to let the patient die. Why, then,' " he continued rhetorically, " 'is it not justifiable to remove food?' "[3]

Why not indeed? The method entails no cost, and actually saves on medical bills since no bill for food need be run up. The method has the further advantage that it may be administered by personnel with no special training: orderlies, candy-stripers, pink ladies, or Servicemaster employees are all competent to withhold food from patients. Yet in the late eighties this was not the method of choice, as it was felt to be tryingly slow. Dr. Arthur Clayton, the author

A NEW BILL OF RIGHTS **Stage Three**

of the book, *The Final Remedy,* confessed his preferences in 1988.

> **I tried withholding food but I found even the most incapacitated patients often resorted to violence against the staff. The clothing of nurses was literally stripped from them as patients begged for what was not in their best interests. Now when the decision has been made to terminate, I personally go in with a smile and a shot.[4]**

The CPI office may want to consider, however, that those shots, with as many candidates as we contemplate for PEAD administrations, may constitute a real drain on the limited health care resource (HCR). Poisons have to be manufactured, and overdoses of morphine may deprive those who need the drug for pain relief. Since air is simply one more life-support resource, along with food, the decision as to which of the more natural techniques to apply is apparent. The removal of air has the real advantage of speed over the no-food technique, since it may take days for a patient to starve but only minutes to smother. The trauma is brief: some thrashing and kicking, and muffled screams may attend the procedure; but much of this can be softened by bringing pillows to bear. And no drugs will have been wasted. I firmly recommend that asphyxiation become the treatment of choice in the hospital locale.

The PEAD program will also embrace candidates who may be at large in society: those with criminal records, the "underclass," or the habitually poor, those whose inability to pass the Citizenship Test—the Dr. Falwells of the world and like fanatics—reveal them to be subhuman, and all PUCs (Products of Unlawful Conception: that is, full-term fetal matter brought to parturition outside of the federal guidelines applicable at that moment). These candidates will be gathered and taken to central locations. Of course all persons in federal penitentiaries would automatically be candidates for PEs, and therefore, because the administration of PEAD procedures will be going on in these locales anyway, subhuman anarchists at large in society will be brought to federal penitentiaries where the authorities will be set up to handle them.

Since no one will be imprisoned in these institutions any more, at least for very long, we may consider changing their names to "R & R Spas." Most of us have known the familiar letters R & R as designating the famous Rest and Recreation areas provided for military personnel. These letters will be updated to refer to "Rectification and Remediation." But the former connotations will still cling to them for a time, helping to solve whatever public relations problems we may have in relation to this. Many citizens might quickly endanger themselves by protests that would prove them noncitizens otherwise. R & R participants in PEAD programs will probably have too much animal vitality about them for one-to-one smotherization. For this reason the showers of these great facilities ought to be hooked up to tanks filled with experimental toxic gasses; in this way the PEAD program can go forward, and render a service to the Defense Department at the same time.

Genetic screening will then be used to monitor all future pregnancies. Amniocentesis and the newly invented (as of 1990) Fren's procedure will be universally administered to pregnant women. Fetal tissue removal must follow any detected anomaly. The mother of a defective fetus will not want to waste one of her "punches," after all. What's more, it will be evident at this point how much of a stake society has in every reproductive decision. To carry a defective fetus to term would be more than cruel since it would only bring into the world a candidate for a PE. As such it would amount to murder on the mother's part. No Moses in the bullrushes fantasies may be entertained, either. A society with identification cards rarely has much of an underground network, as China proves. No, such an action would be viciously antisocial, demonstrating that the mother has an insane disregard for the needs of others in her crowded world.[5] She would only end up turning herself, as well as her ex-utero fetus, into a non-citizen.

Sadly, the government will probably have to bear the expense of the CPI office and its PEAD program long after the initial winnowing of the population. Accidents will occur in the home and on the highways, which will result in hospital locale candidates. Also, while the poor and criminal element will be largely eliminated in the first roundups of the PEAD program, genes of their type will continue to appear for many years to come, causing recessive traits to appear in future generations.

The population will surely see then that human births, while full of meaning to the sentimental, entail even with genetic screening too many potentially costly hazards—one twisted molecule can cause everyone a great deal of bother. During the five years after the first Population Census, sperm and egg donors will be requested to make contributions to government reproductive banks. Enough of such materials will be gathered to repopulate society without the need of human mothers for the next one hundred years. Society as a whole will then vote every year on the proposition of assigning reproduction exclusively to *in vitro* means until enlightened opinion has its inevitable day. That vote will mark the final end of any connection between pleasure (sexual liaison) and responsibility (childbearing).[6] Full entitlement to the last of the new rights will not be possible until this comes to pass, which will be the most fundamental argument for the measure. Eventually, the very integrity of our brave new society will be seen to be at stake.

In Stage III of this proposal, the word "human" would be replaced with the more exact term, Acceptable Sapient Unit (ASU). To be sure, our use of the words "persons" and "human" to replace the archaic "man" and "woman" has moved us in the right direction. But we must acknowledge that deep within lies the last and most fundamental guilty secret our race has harbored. We have struggled mightily with prejudice of all sorts: racism, sexism, homophobia, ageism. But we are as yet massively guilty of the worst form of prejudice of all: specieism. We consistently prefer our own kind to all other animals for no reason at all. Peter Singer, Professor of Philosophy and Director of the Center for Human Bioethics of Monash University in Melbourne, Australia, has made this point with great eloquence.

Once the religious mumbo-jumbo surrounding the term "human" has been stripped away, we may continue to see normal members of our species as possessing greater capacities of rationality, self-consciousness, communication, and so on, than members of any other species; but we will not regard as sacrosanct the life of each and every member of our species, no matter how limited its capacity for intelligent or even conscious life may be. If we compare a severely defective human infant with a nonhuman animal, a dog or a pig, for example, we will often find the nonhuman to have superior capacities, both actual and potential for rationality, self-consciousness, communication, and anything else that can plausibly be considered morally significant.

Only the fact that the defective infant is a member of the species *Homo sapiens* leads it to be treated differently from the dog or pig. Species membership alone, however, is not morally relevant. Humans who bestow superior value on the lives of all human beings, solely because they are members of our own species, are judging along lines strikingly similar to those used by white racists who bestow superior value on the lives of other whites, merely because they are members of their own race.[1]

Here, in this clear and ringing moral challenge by a leading ethicist publishing in a leading American medical journal, we see the scientific attitude that will bring East and West together. We may not find it entirely congenial at once. We may be surprised at how deeply the "religious mumbo-jumbo" has affected even the most liberated of us. But with the poets screaming at us about "yearning" and what not, with Oedipus acting as if having had sex with his female parent were "tragic," with Aeneas bedeviled by a destiny that somehow forbade harmless sexual activity with Dido, with Dante and the entire Judeo-Christian tradition so eager to roast us over the pit of hell . . . well, what we have been up against has been simply unspeakable. We must learn to forgive ourselves. We must look to a new terminology, a new name for *homo sapiens* that is not laden with such cultural baggage: *Acceptable Sapient Unit*. This crucial change will be our strength and our salvation. There will be no guilt attached to it, and none of the illusory self-aggrandizement so characteristic of the mythic and

THE LAST GUILTY SECRET

poetic and religious view of "man" as godlike and noble. We can move beyond freedom and dignity at last.

I propose that a further distinction be made between ASUs who contribute to this document's agenda and those who do not. For the latter, in place of the rather abrupt "subhuman" classification, we may substitute *Non-Acceptable Sapient Unit* (NASU). During the early transition from the traditional system of reproduction, in which individual sets of agents will produce "their own" children, and the last phase of this proposal when our embryo banks take on this chore, these classifications will be administered by the Bureau of Population and Environment on a case by case basis. When the banks start decanting their product, both ASUs and NASUs will be "made to order." This may come as a surprise. It might be supposed that when our embryo banks take over NASUs will cease to come into existence. Not at all. NASUs will be decanted on a large scale. All societies have found it expedient to have work that involves much drudgery assigned to a menial or slave class. It is likely that even in the fully robotocized future not all boring work will be eliminated. We may solve this problem in a way analogous to the expediencies of former times, but without resorting to any oppression whatsoever. To all appearances, many NASUs will look "normal," at least by the standards which now exist; but because specieism will have been eradicated, because humanity itself will no longer exist, it will be quite impossible, by definition, to treat anyone inhumanely.

NASUs will themselves be subdivided into Surviving Fetal Matter (SFMs) and Non-Surviving Fetal Matter (NSFMs, the equivalent of today's aborted

Protein enriched tomorrass derived from Non-Surviving Fetal Matter (NSFM), freeze dried and crystalized will yield a baby formula capable of keeping a billion bellies content forever. will "fetal fryers" be far behind?

babies). We have seen the important role fetal tissue has played in medical research and commerce, but its greatest contribution will come when we start producing NSFM embryos in the systematic way *in vitro* gestation will make possible. The world is hungry. It is particularly hungry for protein, which plays such an important role in cognitive development. Homomass derived from NSFM, when mixed with powdered milk, freeze-dried, and made into crystals, will make baby formula that will be truly magic. With it we will solve the hunger problem of the world's infant population, and at the same time win many more nations to our goal of reduced population growth.

The older members of these societies must not be neglected either. No one will propose that NSFMs be shipped to other countries and eaten whole. Anthropologist Levi-Strauss has shown the academic community how important the distinction between the cooked and the uncooked is to every known society. Therefore NSFMs should be introduced into foods whose preparation and packaging will make the introduction of NSFM meat and meat by-products more acceptable.

When we succeed in exporting the technology and monies needed for NSFM factories, more wholesale uses might be made of NSFMs. The appearance of NSFM flesh under a cellophane wrapper will probably cause no great reaction if it is handled and packaged to look as much like a large fowl as possible. We might call this birdlike food product a "fetalfryer" or a "humanhen."

When humanhens are introduced, as they inevitably will be, in the American supermarket, some, I suppose, may object that such uses of NSFMs smack a little of cannibalism. What if it does? The presence of cannibals in the human community demonstrates that cannibalism has always been a viable option in satisfying nutritional needs. The Judeo-Christian tradition with which we in the West are so burdened has always taken a very dim view of cannibalism, it's true; but once the complete bankruptcy of the Judeo-Christian tradition comes home to our hearts as well as our minds (it's been two hundred years since the Enlightenment, so it's about time), we will see that the notions of a just society and cannibalism are not mutually exclusive at all.

Surviving Fetal Matter (SFMs) will carry out tasks unsuitable to the dignity of ASUs. Six areas of responsibility are projected for them.

First, they will undertake the whole gamut of menial tasks; this will include garbage removal, public latrine cleaning, bedpan duty in hospitals, sewer inspection and repair, and toxic waste disposal. It will also include "shepherding" R & R candidates to their final destination—whatever violence may occur during these trips will then not be directed against ASUs.

Second, some SFMs will be selected to serve as an organized force to bring about just societies in other lands by the methods outlined in this proposal. SFMs will be used especially in places where intense enculturation of the populace is needed before Stage I can go into effect. They will serve as military advisors to guerillas engaged in struggles against oppressors, exploiters, investors, and other enemies of the people. Having been engineered for this purpose, they will have inbred in them an overwhelming urge to bomb, sack, pillage, plunder, rape, and carry out acts of arson without any regard

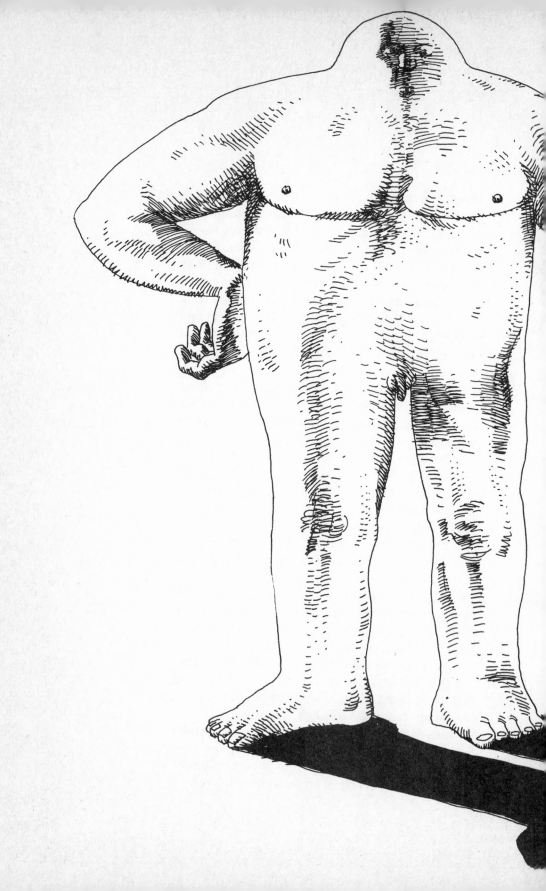

anticipating anxiously a future untrammeled by traditional notions of freedom. Bowing to the historic inevitability of self-destruction, while chanting knowingly "Work makes you free." Our historic appointment with non-being. Kali, your servants await. Ah death where is thy sting?

to their own welfare, all in the cause of peace.

Third, other SFMs will be used in the space program as we once used monkeys; they will ride aboard prototype spacecraft, performing various simple functions, which will enable scientists on the ground to monitor the performance of new equipment. They will also, in this regard, help us conquer the immense distances between the stars, which, due to present propulsion technology, have kept us from exploring regions beyond our own solar system. At this date it would be possible for three SFMs piloting an APB-23 to reach several of the closest stars before their food and water supplies ran out. Their communications equipment might not stand up to the years of traveling before the SFMs themselves would break down, but this is just one of those inevitable risks all great projects must run.

Fourth, they will be employed in the entertainment industry so that the "psychic distance" introduced by stunt men in adventure pictures—the artificiality that limits our pleasure when we know that the car may go over the side of the mountainous road but no one will actually be killed—this distancing will be overcome. SFMs will create the most spectacular car crashes, shoot it out at high noon, be dumped out of airplanes without parachutes, be riddled with machine gun bullets, be hanged by the neck until dead, have their heads chopped off by machetes, by chain saws, by guillotines, and it will all be *as real as an SFM can make it*. Think what the Sam Peckinpahs of our day will be able to create!

Fifth, SFMs will continue to furnish subjects for medical research. New techniques such as brain transplants, high-thermal cancer therapy (in which the subject will be heated for a short period to the limits—about 107 degrees Fahrenheit—of ASU homeostasis), and "build-up" shock therapy will be tested. A special branch of the project will examine biological warfare techniques. Poxes and plagues will be unleashed in control groups varying in size up to one million SFMs. Those sprays (i.e. "yellow rain"), which cause the spontaneous swelling and rupture of every type of membrane in the human body, will be a special focus.

Finally, SFMs will make it possible to grant every citizen the right of unlimited sexual gratification. Single and multiple partners will be engineered to suit every predilection.

This will be the greatest of all blessings. As a necrophiliac, I have suffered uncounted humiliations while attempting to slip into funeral homes and morgues. There is nothing sacred about a "human" body, particularly a dead "human" body.[2] But what misunderstanding and guilt-inducing reactions I have met with in persons with seemingly liberal attitudes! Indeed, many necrophiliacs, because of these difficulties, find their job opportunities curtailed, limited to the positions of mortician and morgue attendant. I, myself, because I have been determined to pursue another career, have resorted to various ruses: I have posed as a medical student; I have concocted a fictional hospital entity through insurance records in order to obtain cadavers for "research"; and I will even admit to acts of breaking and entering.

I include these personal difficulties to show how pervasive prejudice against my sexual preference really is. With the advent of lively or deteriorating SFM use for every sexual appetite, all the skulking about for those with unusual sexual preferences will have ended. Voyeurs will not have to wait in hiding behind their peepholes on public latrines. Pedosadists will not have to conceal their activities from busybody social workers. The 42nd Streets in every major city will have government regulated sex palaces catering to every possible need. These establishments will have the same patina, where it's desired, as, say, Tiffany's, Gucci, or the Palm Court at the Plaza Hotel in New York. The inevitable guilt that follows the disapproving glances of other citizens will vanish when everyone can forthrightly march up to a desk and charge the most unusual of sexual services. (I have found it an absolute law of ASU behavior that no one feels guilty for anything he can put on his Diner's Club, Visa, or American Express card.)

How far reaching, beyond what had once looked to be only one's fondest dreams, are the reforms open to us now.

When we have extended all Acceptable Sapient Units throughout the world the full complement of the old and the new rights, we still may not have guaranteed each citizen success in the pursuit of happiness. I believe this proposal has been, thus far, reasonably thorough in searching out the implications of population control. Still, hard questions remain to be asked. We must admit, in fairness to ourselves and our opponents, that we still have not satisfactorily answered the most fundamental question: what makes an ASU an ASU? Here science must give way to speculation. The following remarks—and this is the only claim I make about them—seem, at least to my mind, to be logically consistent with the rest of this proposal. Nevertheless, I am not sure I have been able concerning this most difficult of questions to rein in my worst self, the poet in me. I readily acknowledge at any rate the ambiguities of this matter of acceptability. Every horizon has its vanishing point.

That said, in the last analysis, what is "acceptability" anyway? The ability to reason, to interact with culture, to participate in creative relationships—these things, certainly. Such attributes and others like them, however, seem to be generated by intellectual faculties which are embued with suffering. While we may dispense with the religious mumbo-jumbo about "man" and come to a fresh perspective on our deepest yearnings, we may still be troubled by that great hope chest, the ASU mind. Pausing from our labors, we may perhaps remember the lover lost more than the lover won. We may reflect upon the destinies of others, which we would in some regards wish to live out ourselves. In these and countless other ways, our imaginations throw up to us a type of poverty, the severe limitations of being one ASU with one life; we must live with the unhappy paradox of being a creature afflicted with an imagination to which nothing seems to be denied, while so much is impossible to the will simply by virtue of our finiteness.

The hope chest of the mind turns out to be a Pandora's box. Out of it leap considerations that even the most devoted utilitarian finds profoundly disturbing. The very fact of our existence often causes us to wonder. Soon our identities and fates will be strictly determined, and so we will know in a fairly satisfactory manner who we are and where we are going. But, why are we here? That question doesn't look to lose its force. On its heel the other questions may return in a subversive form: why did "they" make us this way? why did "they" choose such and such a destiny for me?

Then, too, the most sublime moments in life seem to remind us of we know not what: something in the past, perhaps, or something in the future; some kind of ideal state of which life at its most intoxicating seems to give us but a foretaste. Thus we are nostalgic. Thus we are sentimental. Thus we invest proximate ends with distressingly ultimate expectations.

Finally the mind brings with it self-consciousness, which in turn entails the knowledge of our own death. We speak, we move, we have our being, in the knowledge that we shall soon not speak with our friends, not move to the beat of life's music, not *be*.

Our reforms started out with the objective of eliminating suffering. Suffering may turn out to be, however, an inextricable part of being an ASU. The religious mumbo-jumbo served as a palliative of all

THE CONSUMMATION

this, promising to compensate for present pains with future rewards. The population planner can make no such promises. Certainly many people, myself included, would say that by the severe ascetical discipline of refusing to contemplate the meaning of things we have secured our own type of salvation. But we can't expect such highly spiritual antispiritual rigors of the population at large. Some might suggest, after Plato, that we should compose new myths for the common run of ASUs. Unfortunately, we have educated the populace to be wary of traditional religion. Everyone has the phrase "cosmic accident" on his lips at the least mention of why ASUs came into being. ASUs know that only purposelessness has spawned this creature so enamored or purpose. That meaninglessness has commissioned his search for meaning. That at last chaos will flout compassion, the random vitiate redemption, and chance preside high above choice. It must be clear then that acceptability itself is not only *unacceptable* but *intolerable.*

The concept all our recent progressive programs have been striving so valiantly against, the great enemy to all authentic liberation, the antithesis to this proposal's thesis, is nothing more, nor less, nor other, than *life as an ASU itself.* It is life that teases us with hopes of love and success and achievement and honor, only to snatch away the satisfactions of these things just as we touch them. It is life that sits like a gargoyle, grinning and leering high above us as we struggle through the littered streets of our days. It is life that engenders those impossible hopes, those accursed yearnings.

The consummation of this proposal would then be—insofar as we can presently determine—the annihilation of the benighted ASU race. A bold step, yes. But not any different, really, than what others have proposed. Eastern religion, which is not devoid of sense like our Judeo-Christian tradition, speaks to this issue: life for ASUs *is* an endless round of suffering. Eastern religion came up with a version of our remedy as well; the Buddha taught that the ego must be shattered so that the soul might join in the unity-of-being called nirvana. Of course, nirvana was simply a symbolic way of treating this yearning for annihilation within the human breast. Freud spoke about the same thing in identifying the "death wish." We can be more honest about it than both Eastern religion and Freud, and show greater courage in our concrete actions.

At some point, therefore, embryo decanting procedures must be terminated. A "life-expectancy" warranty should be issued to each of the last *in vitro* products. Upon the warranty's expiration, the holder will report to a designated CPI counseling center to receive a Voluntary Self-Extinction (VSE) vaccination. Her or his body will then be cremated so that the ASU may return to the blissful harmony of the elements.

All shall be well when the last two CPI medical personnel administer VSE vaccinations to each other, and, quickly thereafter, lie down on an automated tractor belt, which will carry them into the purifying fire.

ASU history will thus have what seems to me its only fitting—we might say positive—ending. Nature will have been rid of the creature that has sinned most against her. Whales will sound without fear of fast-running harpoon boats and the floating processing plants which follow. The California condor and the bald eagle will ride ascending heat thermals in unpolluted skies once more. And the long-suffering earth will reach up with vines and tendrils to reclaim the minerals that have been extorted from her to build our tumor-like cities. Slowly the wound of civilization will heal.

In sum, what we might call the "collisions" caused by this cosmic accident, the ASU, the smash-ups which ASUs have had with their own kind and the wrecks they have caused in the world about them, will have ceased. Nature's one and only sin against herself will have been redeemed. And we, for what it's worth, will have taken our revenge against those hopes, those yearnings, by which cruel Chance directed us toward that mirage of the nonexistent Other.

THE BUREAU OF POPULATION
AND ENVIRONMENT
14815 PENNSYLVANIA AVE.
WASHINGTON, D.C.
00100-DF-XXXY3420

FROM THE DESK OF MS. DIANA MARSH
INTEROFFICE MEMO

C.B.:

Your manuscript is eminently reasonable. Its only weakness, I feel, is that your kind nature has led you to be overly solicitous of people's sensibilities. Yes, let's go to lunch and brainstorm. Is Friday O.K.? I can see that a man of your experience is going to be an invaluable asset when sanity triumphs in the nation. As they used to say, same struggle, same fight.

Di

C.B. Train is definitely not a nice person. Unfortunately, many genuinely nice people actually do share his frame of mind. The spirit of our times has led many to accept unwittingly the inhuman ideas upon which coercive population control theory and its ally, eugenics, rest. We have tried to bring the essential nature of these ideas into view by depicting their absurd and brutal implications for mankind.

We are a little worried, however, that what is manifestly absurd to us may sound like common sense to others. The authors found it somewhat difficult to dream up crazier proposals than those the apologists for population control and bioengineering are putting forward in all seriousness. It was even harder to signal by the use of an unusually strident tone, that C.B. Train's thinking was hysterical. The work of Paul Ehrlich is representative in both regards. (His best-selling book, *The Population Bomb*, first issued in 1968 and again in a revised edition in 1971, largely formed the attitude of a generation toward population control.) Take, for example, this shrill passage in which Ehrlich and those he quotes decry leaving family planning up to families rather than the state.

> He [Kingsley Davis] points out that, "The things that make family planning acceptable are the very things that make it ineffective for population control. By stressing the right of parents to have the number of children they want, it evades the basic question of population policy, *which is how to give societies the number of children they need* [our emphasis]. By offering only the means of *couples* [Davis's

emphasis] to control fertility, it neglects the means for societies to do so." Or, as Justin Blackwelder once said, "'Family planning' means, among other things, that if we are going to multiply like rabbits, we should do it on purpose. One couple may plan to have three children; another couple may plan seven. In both cases they are a cause of the population problem—not a solution to it." Above all remember that planned, well-spaced children will starve, or vaporize in a thermonuclear war, or die of plague just as well as unplanned children (p. 79).

This passage is so outrageous that it's hard to grasp at first. Davis, Blackwelder, and Ehrlich by 1971 had accepted in no uncertain terms that the state should dictate, insofar as possible, the number of children that come into the world. The corollary of this proposition, that the state should dictate *what kind* of children come into the world, logically follows. There you have just about everything that C.B. calls for with no apologies. Rather than apologize, Ehrlich wards off any objections with threats of thermonuclear war and the black death. Intimidation isn't the same thing as reasoning, and usually belies distrust by an author in his own argument.

As Ehrlich's ability to quote others on this topic indicates, he is hardly alone in his brave new world designs. As avuncular a figure as Linus Pauling, the Nobel Prize winner, good old Mr. Vitamin C himself, has launched the idea that the genotype of young people should be tattooed on their foreheads so that

young lovers will know not to copulate with someone from the wrong side of the genetic tracks.[1]
James F. Danielli, director of the Center for Theoreti-
cal Biology, on the State University of New York
campus at Buffalo, has come up with a revisionary
version of original sin. Humanists have been telling
us all along that man was only evil because of his
environment. Danielli, and others like him, now believe that the possibility of improving human behavior by improving his environment "is a dubious
proposition" with mankind's present genetic endowment.[2] Instead he looks to bioengineering to
improve human nature. Where once evolution was
a source of hope, the ascent of ape into man, now it
will be a cause of regret: man will be found to have
too many ties to the animal kingdom. Bioengineering will be advocated as the "clean break" from the
animal kingdom that Christians once thought took
place when God breathed the spirit of life into this
creature made in his image. Human beings will be
redefined. They will now become the animal, as C.B.
Train might say, who has bred with a singular regard
for aggressive traits through the millennia. It's easy
to catch C.B.'s voice in all this. Already we have
grown too accustomed to his patter for anybody's
good.

The first chapter of C.B.'s *Proposal* is an extended
exercise in how to lie with statistics. When Ehrlich
and others state that half of the world's population is
mal- or undernourished (a statement that originated
in Ehrlich's *Bomb*, p. 18, and has since become standard), they are not really trying to elicit our sympa-
thy for the poor. Malnourishment afflicts about
10–15 percent of the world's population according

to Julian Simon, a professor of economics at the University of Maryland and the leading opponent of the population bomb mentality. That means about 400 million people don't have enough to eat. All but the Hitlers among us will find more than ample reason for compassion at the thought of 400 million people enduring unnecessary suffering. So why exaggerate?

If we accept that half the people in the world are hungry we will very likely panic. In our fear, we probably will be willing to deliver whatever authority is necessary to those who will *protect us from a similar fate.* Ehrlich & Co.'s appeal is not to humanitarian concern, but to self-interest. (Reading Ehrlich's book we experienced what we feel to be a telltale reaction: the passages about future catastrophes which could wipe out large portions of the world's population came, not so paradoxically, as a relief.)

There is a qualitative as well as a quantitative difference between 10–15 percent and 50 percent of the population. By falsely inflating the dimensions of the problem, Ehrlich & Co., in effect, have created a nonexistent emergency. That millions of people are starving *is* a tragedy. But the false numbers make it appear that we do not have the skill, tools, and natural resources to address this problem. This supposed lack of resources and expertise is a lie. It is meant, consciously or unconsciously, to undermine present institutions within the Western democracies, causing them to default their authority to the population planners. While in our panic we are serving what we may mistake for our own interests, they will be the ones who will actually benefit.

The progress of Ehrlich & Co. in accomplishing

their agenda has been impeded of late by pro-life concerns and the much-advertised return to traditional values. C. Everett Koop, as surgeon general, has called attention to the practice of infanticide in American hospitals. The courts have so far overruled his defense of helpless infants, but at least Koop is there to awaken people to the problem. Even so, from the first publication of Ehrlich's *The Population Bomb* in 1968, through the decade of the seventies, Ehrlich & Co. managed to change the climate of opinon to a remarkable extent.[3] At the time he wrote *The Population Bomb*, Ehrlich was clearly speaking to a public that was basically hostile to his views. As he said, "death control goes with the grain, birth control against it." The public and its leadership were, in his view, sadly pro-life.

One indicator of how much that has changed is the reigning view on what position is most expedient in politics. After the winnowing of the first primaries in the 1984 election, not one serious candidate for the Democratic presidential nomination was pro-life. Ehrlich also called for linking aid to poor countries to the implementation of population control measures. That has not been done. But until just now, our government has chosen to fund international agencies, like AID, whose "relief work" is as much directed to population control as to relieving people of hunger and disease. Social institutions provide another barometer. Ehrlich faulted Planned Parenthood and other family planning groups for standing against abortion. They have reversed their stand. In the schools, most sex education programs have followed his doctrine that thoughts about sexual pleasure should be divorced as far as possible from thoughts about procreation. Ehrlich & Co. have created a climate of opinion that is pro birth control to the point of being antinatal. The August 6, 1984, issue of *Time* magazine had as its title for that week's cover story, "The Population Curse." People are seen now as a "curse," not only by population planners but also by the popular media.

Part of the Christian community finds its weather these days blowing in from this high-pressure front. Catholics, except for renegades like Father Drinan, have recognized the absurdity of Ehrlich & Co. for what it is. The response of the evangelical community has been more of a mixed bag. What often happens in the evangelical community is that the doctrines of the pagans get a quick dunk in the baptistry and then are promoted, like the thoughts of our superstar converts, as authoritative.

This habit of mind is exemplified by Ronald J. Sider's *Rich Christians in an Age of Hunger* (Inter-Varsity Press, 1977). Sider's book consists of a stripped-down version of Ehrlich's population planning argument justified by isolated Bible verses. We must admit that Sider wrote his book when the population planners were at the height of their influence and before the neoconservative critique, which has helped us form our own views, came along. We readily confess that our ideas are not wholly original with us, nor are they found in complete form in the Bible. They are what we take to be extensions of biblical principles. And we recognize that the tone of Sider's book is softer than Ehrlich's. Granted all of that. Yet in the end—and this is the most important thing—*Sider embraces coercive population control measures similar to those Ehrlich espouses.*

To make sure that food aid does not encourage countries to postpone hard political decisions

on necessary agricultural reforms, especially land redistribution and *population control programs*, the United States and Canada should announce that food aid will go only to the countries which are implementing the internationally agreed upon World Plan of Action drawn up at the U.N.'s Population Conference (Bucharest 1974) and the U.N.'s World Food Conference (Rome 1974) [our emphasis] (p. 216).

This statement seems innocuous at first, but let's unpack it and see what it means. In order to make sure that countries institute population control programs, Sider wants us to withhold food aid from nations that refuse to implement population control programs. In other words, to accomplish his ends, he is willing to see these countries starve.

Mankind has never been very good about following Christ's admonition to love our enemies. In times of war we have, however, generally abided by rules which call for medical and other treatment to be given to wounded enemy soldiers. This charitable principle is a hallmark of the Western democracies. Sider apparently rejects this minimal standard of Christian love in the cause of population control. He isn't willing to extend the means of sustenance to nations who find his population control plans misguided, to people who can hardly be worse than avowed enemies. What's more, he discriminates against the greater portion of the Christian community. Any nation that abided by Roman Catholic teaching on birth control would be excluded from the pale of Sider's mercy. Finally, Sider gives implicit support here to the hysterical population measures which brought about forced sterilizations in India and which constitute the most ungodly force in China today. Sider could not have known the reign of terror population planning would bring with it, but his statement is a chilling reminder of the dangers of being a fellow-traveler with a secularist. There are finally two ways to think about Sider's position: either he did not know what he was saying, or he was espousing views that are well-nigh totalitarian.

Many don't know what they think about sanctity of life issues. We encourage you to investigate the matter, using our notes to C.B.'s manuscript as a guide to deciphering the population bomb code. Julian Simon's *The Ultimate Resource*, Julian Simon and Herman Kahn's *The Resourceful Earth*, and Germaine Greer's *Sex and Destiny* are also essential reading on the issue of population planning. *Rites of Life* by Shettles and Rorvik, *The Unaborted Socrates* by Peter Kreeft, *Death in the Nursery: The Secret Crime of Infanticide* by James Manney and John Blattner, and *Rachel Weeping* by James Burtchaell are places to start in understanding the paramount issue of the sanctity of life and abortion. Finally, *Modern Times* by Paul Johnson shows throughout that the genicidal character of the twentieth century comes from attempts at "human engineering."

To those who have investigated the matter, we must say that there is no excuse for anything other than an unequivocal pro-life stand. The evidence shows clearly that human life begins at conception. What's more, abortion in practice has little to do with the hard cases. Infanticide and euthanasia are already paving the way for a world that is not in the least consonant with a Christian vision. Still the authors will admit that taking a pro-life stand isn't easy. We're not exactly cheerful about it ourselves. To live in a country in which thousands of babies are murdered each day with legal sanction is of itself a burden. And then, once anyone admits that there is a silent holocaust going on in this country, one's Christian duty rapidly takes on a new and frightening aspect. The ghost of Dietrich Bonhoeffer, the German pastor who was executed for trying to assassinate Hitler, arises. What indeed is demanded of us?

For now, arguing and voting for a pro-life government, giving aid to young pregnant women who want to keep their babies, marching, picketing, and sitting-in seem to be enough. As the conflict intensifies, however, some will suffer personal injury (there have already been instances of this) and imprisonment. When Thoreau committed his famous act of civil disobedience, a friend asked the poet why he was in jail. Thoreau replied that the more appropriate question, given the injustices of the day, was why his friend was not. Soon that hard question may confront all of us.

The problem of international hunger and related health concerns also asks us, in Mother Teresa's phrase, to give until it hurts. Relief agencies need money, workers, and supplies to address the needs of the hungry in times of crisis. It's remarkable that we have let the population planners seize the high moral ground on this issue when Christians have always been the chief source of worldwide relief. Ehrlich castigates the "do-gooders" for their efforts. But organizations like MAP International, World Vision, World Concern, Food for the Hungry, the Tear Fund, and agencies of the Southern Baptist Convention—as well as the host of Catholic orders and relief agencies—have provided concrete help to millions of people, in distinct contrast to the population planners.

We must also engage in helping poor nations with

problems that do not attract as much attention as shortages of food, but have equally as negative an impact on millions of lives. As Philip Yancey discusses in "Just This Side of Hell," one of the essays in his collection, *Open Windows,* European nations experienced drastic reductions in infectious diseases, like scarlet fever, influenza, and pneumonia, long before the advent of penicillin and immunizing inoculations.[4] Sanitation systems were the key. The greatest pollution problem in the world *is still by far* the disposal of human wastes. It's difficult to raise money for such projects, but it shouldn't be. Water treatment plants are also a must. The World Health Organization estimates that 80 percent of all health problems in the Third World are attributable to unclean water sources. And many times fairly localized famines might be alleviated if there were just adequate roads connecting underdeveloped areas with locales of supply. These sorts of projects deserve generous support, as well as the distribution of emergency food stuffs.

When we consider the underlying causes of these problems, we see that the rapidly expanding populations in some countries attest to one of civilization's limited successes: the rich nations of the world have been able to export enough of their technology to lower mortality rates in poor countries. We have not, however, exported enough of our power to create wealth as yet to help poor countries provide a decent minimum standard of living for their populations. This is the only long range solution for problems related to population expansion. Thus rapidly expanding populations in poor countries *are,* at least in the short term, causing many difficulties. These nations sorely need to go through the demographic transition which reverses the logic of having large families. As long as mortality rates are as high as they still are, poor people in agricultural societies will have large families in order to produce a ready supply of field hands and to insure the security of the older generation as they age. Large families are the oldest form of social security. When parents can expect that each child is likely to live a full, healthy life, then they stop having such large families.

The Western European nations have gone through this demographic transition, and that is why our populations are stable. The population planners in a most condescending way talk as if the poor engage in "untrammeled copulation." The only people who have ever engaged in "untrammeled copulation" have been members of decadent societies, including at present the "liberated" among us who count on birth control and abortion to divorce pleasure from procreation. The institution of marriage and ethical sanctions against promiscuity—particularly when that institution works through arranged marriages—are effective means of population control. These forces will control population growth in countries that are presently poor when the demographic transition is accomplished—unless of course the population planners manage to export their antinomianism.

The long-term solution of the population expansion, then, depends on poor nations learning how to use the technology of the industrialized world to create dynamic economies of their own. Far from being the great exploiters of mankind, the capitalist nations have gone about increasing the wealth of the underdeveloped nations even as they have used the resources of these nations to prosper themselves. (This isn't saying of course that international companies have never paid unfair prices for natural resources.) Despite the rapid increase in population among Third World countries, food production has increased at a rate greater than the population. The absolute numbers of people in these countries suffering from deprivations of food and services has generally either remained the same over the past twenty years or decreased. The percentage of these populations in want have decreased universally. Peter Berger, in the July, 1984, issue of *Commentary* magazine, reflecting on a book he wrote a decade ago, *Pyramids of Sacrifice,* notes that in his now dated work he was much more disposed to accept a socialist economy as a potentially effective means of increasing the total wealth of a nation. Since then he has observed that the great success stories in the Third World—South Korea, Hong Kong, Taiwan, and Singapore—are all nations with capitalist economies. Socialist economies have not only failed to produce abundance, but in addition they have *always* resulted in a gradual loss of human rights and civil liberties. Marx predicted that capitalism would destroy itself; in point of fact, socialism is the system with built-in self-destructive tendencies. See *Equality, The Third World, and Economic Delusion* by P. T. Bauer.

We have all learned to be apologetic about the "cultural imperialism" of missionary work. We should probably reconsider our reservations. Berger points out that his four developing nations not only share capitalist economies but also cohesive cultural backgrounds. Since the Christian consensus that once existed in this country provided the cohesive cultural milieu we needed to create wealth, we may expect that it would serve the same purpose elsewhere. Only Christ provides an adequate basis for helping one's neighbor, a prime ingredient of development. Only in Christianity do we find a view of man that validates the intellectual and moral sovereignty of the individual. Man, in the Christian view, is a creature whose creativity ought to find expression in the business of tending whatever happens to be his own garden. This may be the ultimate support Christianity, by implication, gives to capitalism. Capitalism is usually justified on the basis of making virtue of necessity (i.e. Man is greedy, and capitalism harnesses greed for the good of everyone). It need not be. Marx was right in saying that man should not be alienated from his own labor: he was wrong about the effect of socialism in this regard. In handing the fruits of a man's labor over to a managerial elite, socialism alienates everyone but the members of that elite. (The real issue, as Paul Johnson has argued, is not personal property, but power. Personal property, among other things, is a hedge against too much power being taken over by the state.) Capitalism seeks to reserve as much sovereignty as possible to the individual. When it functions best, it provides a context for business which maximizes that sovereignty with which God endowed man. This is one of those implications of man being made in the image of God that C.B. found "meaningless."

What we see in the designs of the population planners is late Romanticism applied to public policy. The late Romantics found human suffering either inexplicable or the work of a malevolent God. Man could do nothing about his own death, except perform an act of paradoxical redemption by *willing that death*. Man could, in a limited sense, deny the sovereignty of a malevolent God by beating Him to the punch. Suicide to the late Romantics was thus the highest act of morality, a reproach to the malignant deity. The population planners have, consciously or unconsciously, a similar attitude. Their program amounts to this: if death is inevitable, we will administer it. They are in fact in love with death as an act of metaphysical revenge. That is why it is symbolically right that C.B. Train should be a necrophiliac. Late Romantics are all great death-lovers.

Real Christianity takes exactly the opposite view. C.B. is wrong when he thinks that the Christian position amounts to exchanging the sorrows of this life for the joys of the next. This is a crucial and common misunderstanding of Christianity. The life we know in the here and now, is, as God judged it, *good.* Death is the enemy here, in all its forms—the death of lost meaning, the death of sickness, of political oppression, as well as the death of the grave. We are called to fight that enemy. We must begin by acknowledging the sovereignty of God. The unsought answer to that usually rhetorical question, whose life is it anyway? is this: not mine but God's. To say that I am my own, I own my life, and I can do with it what I please is to accept the first principles of hell. The secularist's desire to save his own life finally results, *often by his own desire and action,* in its loss.

But when we view ourselves as the stewards of our lives, God, who created those lives, is able to preserve and keep them. Thereby, we shall gain the only thing we love more than death: that Life which calls to us in our wild yearnings and impossible hopes.

Chapter One

1. Paul R. Ehrlich, *The Population Bomb,* 2nd ed. (New York: A Sierra Club/Ballantine Book, 1971), p. 18. This statistic is refuted by Julian L. Simon, who cites the U.N. figure that 10 to 15 percent of the world lives in "actual hunger." See Julian L. Simon, *The Ultimate Resource* (Princeton, New Jersey: Princeton University Press, 1981), p. 62. Simon goes on to say that even this figure has been criticized, and notes that the definition of malnutrition used in compiling such figures is often vague.

2. Simon, *The Ultimate Resource,* p. 54. The author cites this statistic and others to demonstrate the totally unrealistic nature of most such scare predictions. Not this many people—500 million—suffer even from undernourishment in all of the earth.

3. *The Global Environment and Basic Human Needs,* a report to the Council on Environmental Quality by the World Wide Institute (1978), p. 14.

4. *Ibid.,* p. 17.

5. *Global 2000 Report to the President,* vol. 1 (Washington, D.C.: U.S. Government Printing Office, 1980), p. 17. The actual figure given has been revised to suit the futuristic time period of *Proposal.* It is based on the government report's prediction that food prices will increase "95 percent over the 1970-2000 period." The findings of the *Global 2000 Report* are summarized on the document's first page.

If present trends continue, the world in 2000 will be more crowded, more polluted, less stable ecologically, and more vulnerable to disruption than the world we live in now. Serious

stresses involving population, resources, and environment are clearly visible ahead. Despite greater material output, the world's people will be poorer in many ways than they are today.

It goes on to say:

For hundreds of millions of the desperately poor, the outlook for food and other necessities of life will be no better. For many it will be worse. Barring revolutionary advances in technology, life for most people on earth will be more precarious in 2000 than it is now—unless the nations of the world act decisively to alter current trends.

Julian Simon's *The Ultimate Resource* refutes the reasoning leading to these conclusions. The conclusions themselves are discredited *in detail* by a volume of essays edited by Julian Simon and Herman Kahn called *The Resourceful Earth: A Response to Global 2000* (New York: Basil Blackwell, 1984). In their introduction to *The Resourceful Earth* Simon and Kahn have summarized the findings of the volume's contributors by parodying these paragraphs out of *Global 2000*.

If present trends continue, the world in 2000 will be *less crowded* (though more populated), *less polluted, more stable ecologically,* and *less vulnerable to resource-supply disruption* than the world we live in now. Stresses involving population, resources, and environment *will be less in the future than now* ... The

world's people will be *richer* in most ways than they are today . . . The outlook for food and other necessities of life will be *better* . . . life for most people on earth will be *less precarious* economically than it is now (pp. 1-2).

Global 2000 and *The Global Environment and Basic Human Needs,* the other major text from which the scare statistics in the first chapter are drawn, are two of a kind. Because *Global Environment* shares the same assumptions and methodology of *Global 2000, The Resourceful Earth*'s refutation of *Global 2000* applies equally to *Global Environment*. Simon and Kahn go on to cite the high points of the volume's findings. These cover the ground upon which C. B. Train's *Proposal* is based and related issues, showing that every one of C. B.'s claims in the first chapter is either wholly fictitious or subject to question. Therefore his argument in the first chapter, which is a reasonable facsimile of the population planners' position, turns out to be, as we have said in the postscript, an extended exercise in how to lie with statistics. Since we cannot within this volume's compass refute in detail each of these claims, we have asked for permission to print here the major findings of Simon and Kahn's group.

(1) **Life expectancy has been rising rapidly throughout the world, a sign of demographic, scientific, and economic success. This fact—at least as dramatic and heartening as any other in human history—must be fundamental in any informed discussion of pollution and nutrition.**

(2) The birth rate in less developed countries has been falling substantially during the past two decades, from 2.2 percent yearly in 1964-5 to 1.75 percent in 1982-3, probably as a result of modernization and of decreasing child mortality, and a sign of increased control by people over their family lives.

(3) Many people are still hungry, but the food supply has been improving since at least World War II, as measured by grain prices, production per consumer, and the famine death rate.

(4) Trends in world forests are not worrying, though in some places deforestation is troubling.

(5) There is no statistical evidence for rapid loss of species in the next two decades. An increased rate of extinction cannot be ruled out if tropical deforestation is severe, but no evidence about linkage has yet been demonstrated.

(6) The fish catch, after a pause, has resumed its long upward trend.

(7) Land availability will not increasingly constrain world agriculture in coming decades.

(8) In the U.S., the trend is toward higher-quality cropland, suffering less from erosion than in the past.

(9) The widely-published report of increasingly rapid urbanization of U.S. farmland was based on faulty data.

(10) Water does not pose a problem of physical scarcity or disappearance, although

the world and U.S. situations do call for better institutional management through more rational systems of property rights.

(11) The climate does not show signs of unusual and threatening changes.

(12) Mineral resources are becoming less scarce rather than more scarce, affront to common sense though it may be.

(13) There is no persuasive reason to believe that the world oil price will rise in coming decades. The price may fall well below what it has been.

(14) Compared to coal, nuclear power is no more expensive, and is probably much cheaper, under most circumstances. It is also much cheaper than oil.

(15) Nuclear power gives every evidence of costing fewer lives per unit of energy produced than does coal or oil.

(16) Solar energy sources (including wind and wave power) are too dilute to compete economically for much of humankind's energy needs, though for specialized uses and certain climates they can make a valuable contribution.

(17) Threats of air and water pollution have been vastly overblown; these processes were not well analyzed in *Global 2000* (pp. 2-3).

While the authors of this present work are in no position to verify these findings, nor vouch for the accuracy of the forecasts made by Simon and Kahn's group, we are persuaded absolutely that their arguments are based on sounder premises and are better reasoned than the scare studies of the population planners. We strongly recommend that those interested in these problems read *The Ultimate Resource* and *The Resourceful Earth*.

6. *Global Environment,* p. 17.

7. *Ibid.,* p. 15.

8. See Simon's *Ultimate Resource* for a detailed refutation of Eckholm's influential thesis. In brief, Simon shows that arable land grows—is created from nonarable lands—when demand makes the necessary commitment of resources profitable. The amount of arable land should comfortably meet future projected demands if governmental policies do not stifle the incentive to create such lands (pp. 81-89).

9. *Global Environment,* p. 6.

10. *Ibid.,* p. 6.

11. *Ibid.,* p. 8.

12. *Global 2000,* pp. 2-3.

13. *Ibid.,* p. 2.

14. *Ibid.*

15. Actual figure adjusted from *Global 2000*'s prediction that by "2000 nearly 1,000 billion barrels of the world's total original petroleum resource of approximately 2,000 billion barrels will have been consumed" (p. 39). The percentage given of oil consumed in last thirty-five years is fictitious.

16. *Global Environment,* p. 38.

17. A "wild card" or fictitious reference. Wild cards are scattered throughout the text to meet the demands of the fictional time period.

18. *Global 2000,* pp. 39-40.

19. Quizo is a fictitious character.

20. *Global 2000,* p. 2.

21. Ehrlich, *Bomb,* p. 129.

22. See Michael Novak, *The Spirit of Democratic Capitalism* (New York: Simon & Schuster, 1982), for a refutation of this pervasive but specious argument.

The pattern has been, as Novak shows, that foreign investment ultimately does as much good for the underdeveloped nation as the developed country from which it comes. Many resources, like oil, are worthless without the technology and expertise to put them to use. Thus investments in underdeveloped nations often *create* wealth for these countries that would not exist otherwise. Also, as time goes on, the expertise to develop natural resources is shared so that indigenous ventures may enter into the same enterprise. And generally when this happens, underdeveloped nations have a great advantage in a free market over developed countries in that their labor costs, while they substantially raise the standard of living of the worker, are far less than in developed nations. In sum, international investment tends to balance out standard of living inequities. South Korea is a prime example of this process.

23. See Simon, *Ultimate Resource.* Simon notes that Konrad Lorenz and John B. Calhoun have focused on the breakdown of normal behavior patterns in overcrowded populations of fish, geese, and Norwegian rats. Almost everyone has been exposed to films in which pathetic, catatonic rats are shown. This is one area, however, in which studies with animals have no applicability to human beings. Simon quotes Jonathen Freedman, a former associate of Paul Ehrlich, who concluded:

"Intuitions, speculations, political and philo- sophical theory appear to be wrong in this re- spect. . . . People who live under crowded conditions do not suffer from being crowded. Other things being equal, they are no worse off than other people. . . . It took me and other psychologists working in this area many years to be convinced, but eventually the weight of the evidence overcame our doubts and pre- conceptions" (pp. 254-255).

24. See Simon, *The Ultimate Resource*. Simon shows that both the main tenet of Malthus's argu- ment—that wealth grows by addition, but popula- tion geometrically—and the dismal theorem that growing populations will always eat up any excess wealth are flat out wrong. Malthus himself revised his theory substantially in subsequent editions of his most important work, *An essay on the principle of population, or a view of its past and present effects on human happiness*. Simon suggests that the distortions of the original edition seem to be too useful for the population planners to follow Mal- thus's change of mind.

To put the matter another way: This long run view of demographic history suggests that, contrary to Malthus, constant geometric growth does not correctly characterize the human population. Rather, a major improve- ment of economic and health conditions pro- duces a sudden increase in population, which gradually moderates as the major productive advances and concomitant health improve- ments are assimilated. Then, after the initial surge, the rate of growth slows down until the next big surge. (It was the very large increase in life expectancy that led to the recent population growth in poor countries. Throughout history, life expectancy has hardly changed, compared with the sudden jump during the past few hundred years.) In this view, population growth represents economic success and human triumph, rather than social failure (p. 163).

Simon also addresses Malthus's dismal theorem:

Malthus's theory of population asserts that, because fertility goes up as income goes up, the extra population eats up the extra income—that is, there is a tendency for mankind to be squeezed down to a long run equilibrium of living at bare subsistence. This is Malthus's "dismal theorem." But when we examine the facts about fertility and economic development (as Malthus himself finally did, after he dashed off his first edition) we find that the story does not end with the short-run increase in the birthrate as income begins to rise. If income continues to rise, fertility goes down (p. 184).

Chapter Two

1. The recent advances in knowledge about genetics *do not* affect the ethical questions posed by eugenics, which advocates the selective breeding of mankind in order to improve the race. These ad-

vances only change the *means* by which eugenics might be carried on, but the *ends* to which they might be employed have to be evaluated on the same grounds which applied when Darwin's cousin, Francis Galton, came up with the idea of eugenics in the nineteenth century. In order to know whether the human race ought to be selectively bred we must know *the purpose for which man was created*. Science, in its consideration of any phenomenon, whether it be man, the action of the tides, or supernovas, only investigates *how* these things come into existence, what their constituent elements are, and what affect they have on other things. It never addresses *why* these things came into being. Present evolutionary theory *seems* to address "why" by assuming that all phenomena are the result of chance. But this is, strictly speaking, not a scientific idea—it is outside the purview of science proper. Empirical observation and experiments capable of duplication provide no guide as to whether chance or God supervised creation. Indeed the belief that chance governed creation requires a mighty leap of faith, as more and more scientists are willing to admit. Jeremy Rifkin quotes British zoologist Leonard Matthews: "'The fact of evolution is the backbone of biology, and biology is thus in the peculiar position of being a science founded on an unproved theory—is it then a science or faith?'" *Algeny* (New York: Viking Press, 1983), p. 96. Mathematicians have also computed the probability of simple chance producing life as we know it on earth. Rifkin also quotes Sir Fred Hoyle, the author of *The Nature of the Universe*, who has said that even given the longest possible time periods, the complexity of genetic codes arising merely by chance is about as likely as "'a tornado sweeping through a junkyard . . . [assembling] a Boeing 747'" (Rifkin, p. 127). The belief in chance as the governing hand in the universe is a matter of scientism: a religious faith in theories whose prestige is dependent upon their being associated with science, but which in themselves have no scientific validity. Again, these theories are outside the bounds of the scientific method.

To know whether we ought to employ eugenics, we must answer two questions: 1) Who is man? and 2) For what purpose was he made? We cannot simply base our answer on *what* is man, because it is impossible to derive *ought* (moral imperatives) from *is* (a description of a thing in terms of its constituent elements). The only thing our new knowledge of genetics provides is an expansion of our knowledge of *what* man is made of. When we return to the question of whether we ought to employ eugenics, we must ask ourselves whether eugenics will further the *end* for which man was made. Now if we assume, as those who have faith in scientism do, that man was made for no purpose whatsoever, then we are still obliged to answer what purposes we would *like* him to serve. Here again, science can tell us nothing. The scientism faithful must *choose* the ends to which they would like to devote man, and to do so, they must rely on some system of values. Many like Ehrlich like to pretend that their values are generated by science, but this is a deception. They must choose their values relying on their philosophic outlook, their interpretation of history, and their intuitions of the good. In fact, those in Ehrlich's position must adopt values primarily from intuition, because nothing obliges them to adopt any particular interpretation of history—apart from the logical contradiction of accepting a traditionally religious view—or mandates their philosophic outlook. Christians are in what we would claim to be an entirely different position. We believe God has revealed himself in Christ and the Scriptures, and has thereby *informed* us of the purpose of man.

Finally, an analogy may help us see why the different techniques by which a task is performed do not affect the ethical questions posed by the task itself. Genocide is the systematic destruction of a race. In the early part of this century, the Turks went about the systematic destruction of the Armenian people. They relied on crude methods: swords and guns. When Hitler went about the destruction of the Jews in the Holocaust, he used poison gas—a more sophisticated technique. In both instances, however, the same result occurred: millions died. When we evaluate the ethical questions posed by genocide, the methods employed are not essential to the question. The matter rests on the truth-value of the premises of genocide: whether a race of people is so evil that its obliteration would be a positive good. In the same way, it does not matter whether we conduct eugenics by making sure the nation's citizens are born to cute Aryan couples, or by conjoining the sperm and eggs of Nobel Prize winners in a petri dish. The essential question is the same in both instances: should human beings mandate what kinds of people are born in the future? Our newfound knowledge of genetics suggests that in the near future, we might be able to enforce our will in this matter with greater efficiency: Hitler's use of poison gas enforced his will against the Jews more efficiently than the Turks were able to enforce theirs against the Armenians. But the questions of whether we *ought* to commit genocide or employ eugenics are entirely unaffected by this consideration.

2. The designation "humanlike shapes" derives from the Anglican Church of Canada, Task Force on Human Life, Interim Report, *Dying Considerations Concerning the Passage from Life to Death,* presented to a general synod August 11-18, 1977 (see "Anglican Report in Canada Leans Toward Euthenasia," by Robert Trumball, *The New York Times,* July 28, 1977). Part of the report reads:

Our senses and emotions lead us into the grave mistake of treating human-looking shapes as though they were human, although they lack the least vestige of human behavior and intellect. In fact, the only way to treat such defective infants humanely is not to treat them as human (p. A12).

The Task Force was referring to brain-damaged newborns.

3. All arguments are not equal: this one makes almost no sense whatsoever. Likewise, there are times when the population planners seek to win the day through what amounts to sheer bombast. Take this example from Ehrlich's *Bomb:*

Biologists must promote understanding of the facts of reproductive biology which relate to matters of abortion and of population dynamics. They must point out the biological absurdity of equating a zygote (the cell created by joining of sperm and egg) or fetus (unborn child) with a human being. As Professor Gar-

rett Hardin of the University of California pointed out, that is like confusing a set of blueprints with a building. People are people because of the interaction of genetic information (stored in a chemical language) with an environment. Clearly the most "humanizing" element of that environment is the cultural element, to which the child is not exposed until after birth. When conception is prevented or a fetus destroyed, the *potential* for another human being is lost, but that is all. That potential is lost *regardless* of the reason the conception does not occur—there is no biological difference if the egg is not fertilized because of timing or because of mechanical or other interference (pp. 138-139).

As far as we know, the most favorable environment anyone can imagine will not induce blueprints to grow into a building of themselves. Saying that there is no difference between a sperm and egg and a zygote is like saying that since two sticks rubbed together will produce fire, there is no difference between the two sticks and the fire itself. For the full biological viewpoint, we refer Ehrlich to *Rites of Life* (Grand Rapids, Michigan: Zondervan, 1984) in which the foremost pioneer in human genetic research, Landrum Shettles, shows that from a biologist's viewpoint the conclusion is simply inescapable that human life begins at conception. Shettles also shows that in the abortion debate no biologist has *ever* come forward who would qualify this statement beyond the implantation of the zygote in the womb.

4. Magda Denes, *In Necessity and Sorrow: Life*

and Death in an Abortion Hospital (New York: Basic Books, 1976), p. 247.

5. Doctors Raymond S. Duff and A.D.M. Campbell, "Moral and Ethical Dilemmas in the Special Care Nursery," *New England Journal of Medicine* 289 (October 1973): p. 894.

6. Richard H. Gross, Alan Cox, *et al.,* "Early Management and Decision Making for the Treatment of Myelomeningocele," *Pediatrics* 72 (1983): pp. 450-458.

7. Wild card. Bicksley and his formula are fictitious.

8. Roger Rosenblatt, "The Baby in the Factory," *Time,* February 14, 1983.

9. *The Boston Globe,* June 19, 1984, p. 1.

10. Olga Fairfax, "101 Uses For A Dead (Or Alive) Baby," *The Forum,* January 1984, p. 6. Olga Fairfax is responsible for the one million dollar figure, the half billion dollar figure is a fictitious extrapolation to suit the year, 1992.

11. Hans Perukel "U.S. Government Funded . . . Experiments on Live Aborted Babies," *International Life Times,* November 7, 1980, p. 9.

12. Dr. Lawrence Lawn of Cambridge University's Department of Experimental Medicine, quoted in "Unborn Babies: Critics Being Emotional Says Don," *Cambridge Evening News,* May 18, 1970, p. 11.

13. "From Whose Brains," *Heartbeat* (Spring 1981) p. 18.

14. These tremendous strides were along the following order:

Two years back rumors were heard in Bangkok to the effect that the Vietnamese

were producing new gas mixtures that were capable of deceiving investigators as to their toxic content and their origin. These new substances—it was said—were the result of experiments in a laboratory conducted by a "new Doctor Mengele" [the infamous scientist of the Nazi regime] who operated on human subjects. No one accepted these rumors, which were so clearly "defamatory" to Vietnam. But in April 1982, Adelia Bernard of COER (Catholic Office for Emergency Relief to Refugees), was secretly taken to Phnom Penh where, thanks to a person who worked at the Hôpital Sovietique, she was informed of the incredible truth. The experiments were taking place, in that very hospital as well as elsewhere, and were being conducted on healthy children ranging from two to ten years of age. The children were kept in special homes and during the experiments were placed in transparent plastic spheres equipped with two valves, one for oxygen, the other for the gas that was being tested. There were approximately one hundred children guinea pigs in the area of the hospital alone, while many others lived in laboratory camps built on the tiny islands of the Mekong. The latter were injected with toxic substances.

Incredulous, Mrs. Bernard asked for proof, and after negotiating the payment of $300, her interlocutor entered the hospital and returned with a plastic sphere, with valves and tubes, inside of which lay the dead body of a three-year-old baby. Adelia Bernard put the sphere in a sack and carried it back to Bangkok, where she deposited it on the desk of Mark Brown,

representative of the UN High Commission for Refugees. Brown did nothing, and no "case" was opened.

Lucio Lami, "Yellow Rain, the Conspiracy of Closed Mouths," *Commentary* 76 (October 1983): p. 61.

15. We have just reviewed documentation, the film, *Conceived in Liberty*, that shows graduate students at a major American university testing the sensitivity to pain of human fetuses. The film shows these students stabbing live aborted fetuses with a pin-like instrument until they die. Nothing, we are sad to find, is unthinkable any longer, even in the United States. This landmark documentary film is available from American Portrait Films, 1695 West Crescent Ave., Anaheim, California 92801.

16. This is in fact the direction in which research is headed. Dr. Robert Edwards, a research physiologist at Cambridge University, has been working with "spare" human embryos. In the October 2, 1982, issue of *The Economist*, he writes:

It might become possible and desirable to grow spare embryos to the stage at which tissue cells begin to differentiate . . . The spares might be kept viable in a deep freeze and so provide "spare part tissue" for transplants. An even more awesome future possibility would be the cloning of human embryos. All that is, at present, in the realm of science-fiction rather than fact. But so were test tube babies a few years ago (p. 18).

17. Olga Fairfax, "101 Uses."
18. Michele Vink, "Abortion and Birth Control in

Canton, China," *The Wall Street Journal*, November 30, 1981, p. 26.

19. "'Birth Control' in Red China: Grim Numbers Game," *Human Events*, May 12, 1984, p. 12.

20. "Paying for Abortions," *The Wall Street Journal*, April 9, 1984, p. 34. President Reagan has decided (July 1984) to stop U.S. contributions to organizations like the UNFPA, which fund China's and other coercive population control plans. So the ten year extrapolation may, we hope, turn out to be fictitious.

Chapter Three

1. Jeremy Rifkin in collaboration with Nicanor Perlas, *Algeny* (New York: Viking, 1983), p. 74. We are indebted to Rifkin's *Algeny* throughout chapter 3 for his treatment of the current revisions of evolutionary theory and how this may feed into the bio-engineering revolution.

2. Evolutionary theory is breaking down. Dr. Colin Patterson, senior paleontologist at the British Museum of Natural History in London, has admitted its bankruptcy. Rifkin quotes:

> **"Last year I had a sudden realization. For over twenty years I had thought I was working on evolution in some way. One morning I woke up and something had happened in the night; and it struck me that I had been working on this stuff for twenty years and there was not one thing I knew about it. That's quite a shock, to learn that one can be misled so long . . . So for the last few weeks I've tried putting a simple question to various people and groups of**

people . . . Can you tell me anything you know about evolution, any one thing, any one thing that is true? All I got was silence . . ." (p. 93).

About the evolution of one species into another, Rifkin quotes Dr. Pierre P. Grasse, one of the world's greatest biologists, ex-President of the French Academy of Sciences.

"From the almost total absence of fossil evidence relative to the origin of the phyla [the primary divisions of the animal kingdom], it follows that any explanation of the mechanism in the creative evolution of the fundamental structural plans is heavily burdened with hypotheses. . . . The lack of direct evidence leads to the formulation of pure conjectures as to the genesis of the phyla; we do not even have a basis to determine the extent to which these opinions are correct" (p. 102).

Rifkin quotes David Raup, curator of the Field Museum of Chicago, on the same matter:

"Most people assume that fossils provide a very important part of the general argument in favor of Darwinian interpretations of the history of life. . . . Well, we are now about 120 years after Darwin, and knowledge of the fossil record has been greatly expanded. . . . Ironically, we have *even fewer examples* of evolutionary transition than we did in Darwin's time" (p. 103).

We might anticipate some fun, watching all those

who have taken a condescending attitude about be-lief in the book of Genesis try to explain the inconsis-tencies of their own faith. But the revolution in evolutionary theory looks to go unannounced, until a revised version can be substituted. A great deal of power is at stake, not only for the evolutionary the-orists themselves but also for the institutions in this culture—including the media—who have bought into the evolutionary frame of mind. It's a terrible irony that the most pompous denunciations of the "creationists" have come at a time when the evolu-tionists themselves are in a quandary.

3. On the face of it, the "punctuated equilibria" theory appears to be an argument from silence.

4. Here we have an interesting bit of possible rea-soning. On the basis of a discredited theory, propped up from an argument from silence, C.B. asserts the validity of bioengineering.

5. It does appear that such "enhancements" of genetic endowment may be on the way. Like so many other things, these enhancements will proba-bly be used before anyone thinks about the ethics of the matter, and then we will be told to accept it as a *fait accompli*.

6. Christian ethics certainly do not "fall silent" by virtue of technological innovation. Christ did not say anything about gunpowder, the automobile, or lasers—He didn't say *anything* about technology per se—yet we can derive a Christian view of the uses of these things from the ethical principles He gave us. Bioengineering is no different. Again, the advent of new means does not significantly affect arguments about ends.

7. William B. Provine, "Choosing our Genes," *Hard Choices* (from the accompanying magazine to

the film series produced by KCTS/9, University of Washington, Seattle, WA, 1980), p. 9.

1. C.B. is choosing his ends while pretending everything is dictated by science. He says, "In designing nature we will of necessity arbitrate the specific ends or purposes of all we create . . . ." Then he seems to completely forget what he has just said and advances his religious faith—scientism—in the disguise of true science. C.B. hides his own values like the con man with his white pea under the quickly-shuffled cups.

2. Edward O. Wilson, *Sociobiology: The New Synthesis* (Cambridge, Mass.: Belknap Press of Harvard University, 1975), p. 562.

3. See C.S. Lewis, *The Abolition of Man* (New York: Macmillan Publishing Co., 1947), for a full discussion of this error. Basically one can point out that the proposition, "statements that cannot be empirically verified . . . are meaningless," is self-contradictory. This proposition itself cannot be empirically verified, and therefore it must be meaningless. Human beings have a great deal of experience apart from the kind of empirical experience one can duplicate in a laboratory. To deny history, the world of ideas, and our emotional life the status of evidence is drawing the definition of "experience" in such a limited way as to be prejudicial. It's an all too convenient way to dismiss religion. Fortunately so much gets axed with it that very few accept this proposition when they think about it.

4. We are indebted for the comparison between a Renaissance painting and a blown-up photograph

of a computer chip to a ten-part Time/Life film, *Connections*, which was produced in cooperation with the BBC and narrated by James Burke. It premiered on PBS in the winter of 1979–1980. C.B.'s treatment of the subject is not much more simple-minded than the closing remarks of the film's narrator.

5. Paul Johnson, *Modern Times* (New York: Harper & Row, Publishers, 1983), p. 382.

6. Daniel C. Maguire, *The New Subversives: Anti-Americanism of the Religious Right* (New York: Continuum, 1982), pp. 65–66, 140. Maguire is not alone in these views. Flo Conway and Jim Siegleman in their book, *Holy Terror* (New York: Doubleday, 1982), evaluate the new visibility of fundamentalism in the following passage:

> As we moved out of Washington, we were struck by the speed with which Holy Terror has spread across the country since 1980. Flushed with success, the national leadership of the fundamentalist right appears to have cemented its hold upon its constituency, unleashing a spate of local affiliate organizations and countless spinoffs that are now replicating the movement's goals and methods at state and local levels. Many of these groups have launched their own moral crusades, using the same strategies of manipulation and preying upon the same deep-seated fears, prejudices, and resentments that have proven so effective at the national level. Reaching across the country today, Holy Terror has leaped beyond politics. It is religion run amok: in the battle over abortion and women's

rights, in the teaching of evolution and in the business of elementary, secondary, and higher education, in the news and entertainment media, in religious broadcasting and new fields of mass communications technology, in every faith and denomination, across the spectrum of American culture—and beyond into even larger spheres (p. 9).

7. Wild card. This fictitious quote expresses, we think, how many Christians feel about the *style* of Falwell and Robertson: they would "like to think" they have more in common with a fair-minded liberal than these evangelists. A moment's reflection, however, will tell us that all Christians share the essentials of their faith with Falwell and Robertson, and thus, albeit it's unfashionable, we must recognize our solidarity with them. Reservations about style, misgivings about a reactionary aesthetic taking hold again in the Christian world, these things and related issues are important. In comparision with the atonement of Christ, though, they are mighty puny indeed. Maguire, Conway, and Siegleman know which side they are on, and we must be prepared to accept derision from such quarters rather than deny our Christian brothers.

8. Mary Daly, *Beyond God, the Father: Toward a Philosophy of Women's Liberation* (Boston: Beacon Press, 1973), as quoted by J. Jackson, *No Other Foundation* (Westchester, Illinois: Crossway Books), p. 96.

9. That "wall of separation" between church and state seems to have a secret panel which allows unlimited entry by the state into the church's affairs, as the rest of the passage goes on to demonstrate.

10. The American Home Economics Association's draft of a new definition of the family, in relation to President Carter's White House Conference on Families, as quoted in Burton Pine's *Back to Basics* (New York: William Morrow and Company, 1982), p. 145.

11. "A Proposal for Pedophile Groups," *NAMBLA Journal* (July 1, 1979): p. 5, as quoted in Enrique T. Rueda's *The Homosexual Network* (Greenwich, Conn.: Devin-Adair, 1982), p. 215.

12. *Ibid.*

13. Andre Lord, "When Will the Ignorance End," *Gay Insurgent* 6 (Summer 1980): p. 13, as quoted in Rueda, p. 229.

14. Wild card.

15. Edward O. Wilson, *Sociobiology*, p. 562.

16. Note that the first question in the citizenship test is based upon Ehrlich's definition of humanness, the ability of a person to "interact with culture." We can only wonder, on the one hand, whether mothers are then a part of culture so that the quickening of babies constitutes "interaction," or, on the other hand, whether "interaction" does not come about until after the child detaches himself from his family, becoming a self-supporting adult. From conception to death, human life is a continuum. Definitions like Ehrlich's fail because there are no clear points of demarcation on that continuum.

Chapter Five

1. Although these coercive measures may sound farfetched, they are in line with the opinions of many influential people and do not go much beyond

what some have proposed. For example, Kingsley Davis has said, "Over-reproduction—that is, the bearing of more than four children—is a worse crime than most and should be outlawed." (Kingsley Davis, as quoted in Simon's *The Ultimate Resource*, p. 311.) Ms. Martha Willing, Coordinator of Population Dynamics in Seattle, in a book entitled *Beyond Conception: Our Children's Children* (Ipswich, Mass.: Gambit Press, 1970) has proposed that the state should "penalize deliberate violations of the small family norms and set up controls which prevent such violations." She also specifies what these controls might be:

> **After the third child is born, both mother and father will have to present themselves at a hospital to undergo sterilization procedures. If a couple does not appear, there will be no birth certificate issued to the child, but instead a "third child paper." The mother can be tattooed or marked to signify a third birth to any subsequent doctor. Instead of the missing parent, the child can be sterilized on the spot, insuring that this *undue share of the gene pool* will not be carried foward (p. 174, our emphasis).**

2. Dr. Joseph Fletcher, *American Journal of Nursing* 73 (April 1973): p. 673.

3. Susan Tifft, "Debate on the Boundary of Life," *Time*, April 11, 1983, p. 69.

4. Wild card.

5. The proponents of population control can be very matter of fact about curtailment of civil rights being necessary to their programs. In *The Ultimate Resource*, Simon quotes Willing on this matter.

"In conditions of scarcity the civil right to have unlimited births simply does not exist. Such a claim is attention-getting and suspect. It is a favorite argument of minorities in support of their own overproduction of births. The right to have children fits into the network of other rights and duties we share and must dovetail with the rights of others. When all of us must curtail our production of children none of us has an overriding civil right of this kind. The closer we live together and the more of us there are, the fewer civil rights we can exercise before they infringe upon those of another. This adverse relation between dense population and personal freedom is easily documented around the world. It is time for people sincerely interested in civil rights to expose such special pleading and to intervene when it is leveled against local or national programs" (p. 340).

6. The separation of sexual pleasure from its natural end, procreation, is one of the goals Ehrlich's *Population Bomb* proposed for the sex education classes he envisioned, and indeed, helped bring about.

By "sex education" I do not mean courses focusing on hygiene or presenting a simple-minded "birds and bees" approach to human sexuality. The reproductive function of sex must be shown as just one of its functions, and one that must be carefully regulated in relation to the needs of the individual and society. Much emphasis must be placed on sex as an interpersonal relationship, as an important and extremely pleasurable aspect of being human, as mankind's major and most enduring recreation, as a fountainhead of humor, as a phenomenon that affects every aspect of human life. Contrary to popular mythology, sex is one of our *least* "animal" functions. First of all, many animals (and plants) get along without any sex whatever. They reproduce asexually. It is clear from biological research that sex is not primarily a mechanism of reproduction; it is a mechanism that promotes variability. In many organisms which do have sexual processes, these processes occur at a stage in the life cycle that is not the stage at which reproduction occurs. [If anyone can tell us what this last sentence means, we would be obliged.] And, of course, no other animal has all of the vast cultural ramifications of sex that have developed in human society. In short, sex, as we know it, *is a peculiarly human activity*. It has many complex functions other than the production of offspring. It is now imperative that we restrict the reproductive function of sex while producing a minimum of disruption in the others (p. 134).

Chapter Six

1. Peter Singer, "Sanctity of Life or Quality of Life?" *Pediatrics* 72 (July 1983): p. 128-129.
2. If this seems overdone, consider feminist ideology concerning rape. Feminism insists that rape is not a sexual crime; that it is a crime of violence. This

is like saying that a Marxist revolution cannot be characterized as a war because it is motivated by a desire for a real and lasting peace. If two armies are firing bullets at one another, what you have is a war. The intent of one army (the Marxist army) does not affect the basic character of the action it is carrying out. In the same way, a rapist may be motivated solely by a will to terrorize and humiliate his victim; that's what he usually succeeds in doing. But as his will and intent are accomplished through violent sexual intercourse, his action is undeniably sexual in character. The doublespeak of feminist ideology on this point betrays a hidden agenda: much of feminist thinking has been devoted to establishing the legitimacy of lesbianism. After all, lesbianism, feminism says, is simply one more sexual preference, just like heterosexuality. What happens, however, if the rapist claims that the way in which he prefers to have sex is "one more sexual preference"? Secular feminism can only answer this question by denying the manifestly sexual character of rape. It does everything in its power—to the point of absurdity—to eliminate the very category, sex crime.

The passion with which feminism has maintained this party line indicates its commitment to a *totally* non-judgmental view of sexuality. If anything goes between two consenting partners—including adults having their way with children—why should an act which involves the consent of only one partner pose ethical questions? The necrophiliac's corpse is only a "marital aid." Portnoy used liver; C.B. wants to use Laverne. What's the difference? *There can't be any to the consistently secular mind.*

Postscript

1. Ted Howard and Jeremy Rifkin, *Who Should Play God?* (New York: Dell Publishing Co., Inc., 1977), p. 81.
2. *Ibid.*, p. 82.
3. Simon in *The Ultimate Resource* provides the following example of how influential Ehrlich and others have been.

As a recent example of how much clout the population lobby can muster, consider this list of organizations—with many millions of members—that are on record as supporting H.R. 5062, a bill now (July 1980) before Congress that would create an Office of Population Policy with the aim of achieving zero population growth: the Arizona Family Planning Council; the American Public Health Association; Concern; the Conservation Foundation; Defenders of Wildlife; Environment Action; the Environment Fund; the Hawaii State Commission on Population and the Hawaiian Future; the Izaak Walton League of America; the Los Angeles Regional Family Planning Council; the National Alliance for Optional Parenthood; the National Audubon Society; the National Family Planning and Reproductive Health Association; the National Parks and Conservation Association; the National Wildlife Federation; the Natural Resources Defense Council; the Population Action Council; the Population Crisis Committee; the Population Institute; the Population Reference Bureau; the Sierra Club; the Texas Family Planning Association; the World Population Society; Zero Population Growth (p. 300–301).

4. Philip Yancey, *Open Windows* (Westchester, Illinois: Crossway Books, 1982), p. 56.

Acknowledgments

We would like to thank Tom Howard for his work on the manuscript. He made a crucial contribution to the project, and we stand very much in his debt.

Our thanks go also to Steve Baer who helped us with our research. To Randy Cobler who keyboarded the text and its revision. To Martha Myers of MAP International for providing us with additional information. And we are grateful to Gordon College and Gordon-Conwell Seminary for the use of their library facilities.

Finally, our salute to Swift.